ST. MARTIN, ST. BARTS & ANGUILLA

ALIVE!

2nd Edition

Harriet Greenberg & Douglas Greenberg

HUNTE

D1418042

HUNTER PUBLISHING, INC.
130 Campus Drive, Edison, NJ 08818
☎ 732-225-1900; 800-255-0343; Fax 732-417-1744
comments@hunterpublishing.com

IN CANADA:
Ulysses Travel Publications
4176 Saint-Denis, Montréal, Québec, Canada H2W 2M5
☎ 514-843-9882, ext. 2232/fax 514-843-9448

IN THE UNITED KINGDOM:
Windsor Books International
The Boundary, Wheatley Road, Garsington
Oxford, OX44 9EJ England
☎ 01865-361122; Fax 01865-361133

ISBN 1-58843-356-0
© 2003 Alive Travel Books, Ltd.

Maps by Kim André, © 2003 Hunter Publishing, Inc.
Cover photo: Carlo Villoch/BCI USA
Back cover: Philipsburg (Sint Maarten Tourist Office)

2   3   4

Contents

About the Authors

Harriet Greenberg has been an avid world traveler and accomplished travel writer for over 20 years. She is the author of the award-winning *Israel On Your Own*, as well as other guides in the Alive series. She is currently researching *Puerto Rico Alive*, to be published next year.

Douglas Greenberg graduated from Arizona State University with a degree in Travel & Tourism. He is a public relations executive in New York when he isn't exploring restaurants and nightlife on Caribbean islands.

About the Alive Guides

Reliable, detailed and personally researched by knowledgeable authors, the Alive series was founded by Harriet and Arnold Greenberg.

This accomplished travel-writing team established the renowned bookstore, **The Complete Traveller**, at 199 Madison Avenue in New York City.

We Love to Get Mail

This book has been carefully researched to bring you current, accurate information. But no place is unchanging. We welcome your comments for future editions. Please write us at: *St. Martin & St. Barts Alive*, c/o Hunter Publishing, 130 Campus Drive, Edison, NJ 08818, or e-mail comments@hunterpublishing.com.

St. Barts

Dreams of Caribbean getaways usually start at the first sign of ice on the windshield of your car. As you stand there scraping it away, you realize there will be many days like this in the months ahead. The thought of a winter respite starts to take hold.

The Caribbean islands, whether US, British or Dutch, offer sunny skies, sandy beaches, active sports, good shops and resort hotels. Unless you have a personal favorite based on past experience, any island will do as long as the airfares and hotel rates are manageable. Only a few islands, such as Jamaica, Puerto Rico and Trinidad, have individual cultures that make them appealing. Add St. Barts to that short list. This is a French island that marches to its own beat, and those in the know want to keep it that way.

No splashy advertisement campaigns lure visitors to St. Barts. Instead, people learn about its charm by muted word of mouth. And even that's done subtly, as the people who've vacationed here for years don't want to share their tropical secret. They bemoan the fact that tourism on the island has increased dramatically. Invariably mentioned in the traditional Caribbean guidebooks that touch on every island, and in the literature distributed by the French

West Indies Tourist Offices, are the Rockefellers, Rothschilds and Fords, all of whom own villas on St. Barts. It's little wonder that St. Barts is often referred to as "St. Tropez in the Caribbean." These are not big inducements to vacation here, particularly if you've been to St. Tropez lately.

Growth on the island must be kept in perspective. St. Barts today is what St. Tropez was like before Bardot made it famous. It's true that new hotels and villa communities have been built, but none is high-rise, none has even 100 rooms, and all are locally owned and managed. All are at the deluxe end of the price spectrum. Although cruise ships now anchor in Gustavia's harbor, there is never more than one a day; the number of arrivals is strictly limited. The island is a duty-free port with wonderful boutiques that, though limited in number, offer a wide variety of merchandise. Still, the shops close precisely at noon, not to reopen until 2:30 pm, while the staff enjoys a leisurely lunch. They are not open at all on Sundays.

St. Barts has all the things that have traditionally drawn people to the Caribbean. It has glorious beaches – over 20 of them. The windier part of the island offers great surfing, windsurfing and sailing, while the calmer waters allow for swimming, snorkeling and water skiing. All these activities – as well as organized scuba trips and day-sails – are part of the scene. Additionally, St. Barts has the best restaurants in the Caribbean (although French St. Martin will dispute this). French-trained chefs have added Creole, Thai, Spanish and even cheeseburgers to their traditional French dishes. There are over 50 restaurants to choose from on this small island.

Will you pay a premium to vacation here? Yes, because you are getting more than secluded beaches, small posh hotels and great restaurants. You are paying for the special quality of this unique getaway. Only you can decide if it's worth it.

The Island's Name

The name of the island is Saint Barthélemy. It is referred to by traditional islanders as St. Barth, and by more contemporary islanders as St. Bart or St. Barts.

Getting There

By Air

 There are no non-stop flights from the US, Canada and Europe to St. Barts. Most North American visitors fly directly to Princess Juliana Airport on Sint Maarten, where several commuter lines make the 15-minute flight to St. Barts. Tiny **Gustav III Airport** can handle only 20-seat

Planes can land on St. Barts only in daylight.

"puddle jumpers." The plane heads right at a mountain (called La Tourmente), clears it by an inch, and then drops steeply to the runway. The flight is not for the squeamish. The landing strip, the shortest in the Caribbean, ends at the sea.

An alternative is to fly into Puerto Rico or St. Thomas and connect with a commuter plane there. European carriers fly to Guadeloupe, where passengers connect to the commuter lines. If you are staying on the French side of St. Martin, you can take a commuter plane from L'Espérance Airport near Marigot.

The main US carrier to Sint Maarten is **American Airlines** (☎ 800-433-7300), with daily flights from Miami or Puerto Rico. Continental Airlines and USAir are also good choices.

🔲 TIP

Reserve your commuter airline flight at the same time you make your long-distance reservation. It is imperative to reconfirm your return flight on these commuter lines.

There are usually commuter flights every hour from 7 am till 5:30 pm (later in summer). The commuter airlines serving St. Barts are:

Winair . . . . ☎ 590-27-61-01
Air St. Thomas . . . . ☎ 590-27-71-76
Air Caraïbes . . . . ☎ 590-27-61-90
St. Barth Commuter . . . . ☎ 590-27-54-54

St. Barts

By Boat

Those uncomfortable on small planes have a delightful alternative. Ferries and catamarans connect Sint Maarten/St. Martin with St. Barts daily. The boats are good-sized and modern. It is a lovely ride, taking about one hour from Philipsburg (Dutch) and a half-hour longer from Marigot (French).

The **Voyagers** (☎ 590-27-54-10) offer daily crossings from Marigot (French) at 9 am and 6:15 pm. The trip takes 1½ hours and is a lovely ride that skirts the Dutch-side shore. There is indoor seating as well as sundecks. The return from Gustavia takes one hour and skirts the French coast. Return trips are scheduled at 7:15 am and 4:30 pm. The fare is $50 round-trip. The phone number in St. Martin is ☎ 590-87-10-68; in Sint Maarten, ☎ 599-542-40-96.

The waters are sometimes choppy but never terribly rough.

Oyster Lines (☎ 590-87-46-13) connects Dutch Sint Maarten with St. Barts. The ship leaves from Captain Oliver's Marina for the 45-minute sprint across open waters. Ships leave the marina at 8:30 am and 4 pm and return at 9:45 am and 5:15 pm. Round-trip fare is $48.

Entry Requirements

US and Canadian citizens need a valid passport or a birth certificate and a photo ID. French and

EU citizens need a national identity card. All passengers need a return or on-going ticket.

Customs

US Customs

Items purchased in St. Barts fall under the standard $600 duty-free allowance per person. Handicrafts or works of art made on the island are not subject to duty.

Canadian Customs

Canadian citizens can return with $500 Canadian worth of merchandise if they have been out of the country for seven days.

Departure Tax

There is a departure tax of US $12 when flying from Princess Juliana Airport to St. Barts. A $5 tax is charged those leaving by boat.

Telephones

The area code for St. Barts is 590. If you are calling while on the island, drop the area code and dial only the six-digit phone number.

> **▣ TIP**
>
> When dialing from the US you must dial 590 twice to reach St. Barts. It goes like this: ☎ 011-590-590 + the six-digit number.

Getting Around

From the Airport

Most hotels offer free **airport shuttle service**. Notify them of your flight times and they will meet you there. This is also true for those arriving by boat.

All of the major international **car rental** companies have desks at the airport.

Taxis, which are unmetered, meet every flight. Fix the rate before leaving the airport and keep in mind that fares can add up quickly .

Navigating the Island

◙ TIP

There is no public transportation on St. Barts. A few private
buses operate, but their routes
do not cover the entire island.

Car/Jeep Rentals

We urge you to rent a car for at least part
of your stay. This will give you time to
explore at your own pace and to return to
those spots you enjoy most. Hotels, restaurants
and beaches are scattered all over the island
and you cannot walk from one to the other easily, except in Gustavia. A valid driver's license
and major credit card are required to rent.

The most popular rented vehicle is a jeep,
because roads, while paved, are poorly maintained and the island is mountainous. They
normally have stick shifts, but can be rented
with automatic drive as well. A four-wheel-drive
vehicle is not a must.

International rental companies have airport
desks. They include:

*You can also use
the toll-free
numbers (look in
the* Yellow
Pages*).*

Avis . . . . ☎ 590-27-71-43
Budget . . . . ☎ 590-27-66-30
Hertz . . . . ☎ 590-27-71-14
Europcar (National) . . . . ☎ 590-27-73-33

There are many local agencies as well, several of which are associated with hotels. Inquire at the front desk to see if your hotel also rents cars. These include:

Turbe. . . . . ☎ 590-27-71-42

Gumbs . . . . ☎ 590-27-75-32

Chez Beranger . . . . ☎ 590-27-89-00
(also rents cycles and scooters)

▣ TIP

Make reservations well in advance for high season.

Motorbike Rentals

Motorcycles and scooters are very popular on the island. Rates are about $30 per day. Agencies include:

Tropic All Rent. . . . . . . ☎ 590-27-64-76

Dennis Dufau. . . . . ☎ 590-27-70-59

Chez Beranger . . . . ☎ 590-27-89-00

Taxis

Taxis are available but not very practical. Privately owned, they are scarce on Sundays, holidays and after 8 pm. They do not have meters. There are taxi stands. In Gustavia, ☎ 27-66-31; in St. Jean, ☎ 27-75-81. No tip is expected.

Gas Stations

There are only two gas stations on the island. The larger is near the airport in St.
Jean. It closes at 5 pm each night and is
closed all day Sunday. You can use a major
credit card at the pump here. The smaller
station is in Lorient. It keeps the same
hours and does not accept credit cards.

◙ TIP

You need a debit card with a
pin number to use the pumps
when the gas station is closed.

Orientation

St. Barts is an eight-square-mile island.
It's 4,340 miles from Paris, 1,550 miles
from New York and 20 miles from St.
Martin. It is home to 6,000 permanent
residents, most descended from the original
Norman, Breton and Swedish settlers.
Newcomers include French citizens who have
opened hotels, restaurants and shops here.
Many young French men and women spend a
year or two working in the hotels, restaurants,
shops and watersports centers.

There are lots of interesting attractions and
historical sites on this tiny island. Each is small
and can be explored in a short time. The pictur-

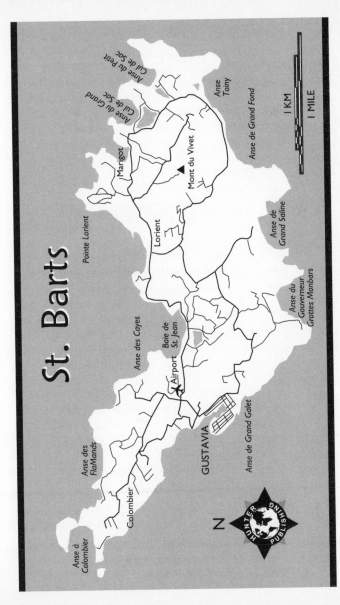

St. Barts

esque towns, some with historical interest, can't help but be adjacent to one of the island's 20 beach strips – nothing is more than five minutes from the sea.

One main road covers the northern tier of the island, with smaller roads leading inland to villages and beaches on the less-developed southern shore.

Towns

We'll pinpoint the main towns here, but you'll find more detail about them and the beaches in the *Sunup to Sundown* section, page 22.

Gustavia

The capital, on the island's southwestern coast, is a picturesque town laid out around a beautiful harbor, which is usually filled with luxury yachts. It has a mini-mall, boutiques, fine restaurants and bars, historic churches and fort, and even a deluxe hotel. The historical Wall Museum is on La Pointe, the peninsula side of the harbor. There are residences in the higher elevations of the town. Key streets include: **Quai de la Républic** and **rue Charles de Gaulle** (the two important commercial streets) and **rue du Centenaire**, the street that connects the two harbor legs.

St. Jean

Located mid-island and on the northern shore, St. Jean is the second-largest town and can almost be described as bustling. Tiny Gustav II Airport is here and there are several small shopping centers. St. Jean Beach is the longest and most popular beach on the island, so there are several hotels and restaurants on or near it. Lovely villas sit above the town on nearby hillsides.

Lorient

Even smaller than St. Jean, Lorient is at the junction of the main road and the road to the island's south shore. It has a school, a mini-market, one of the two gas stations on the island, and two interesting cemeteries. Lorient Beach offers the island's best surfing.

Corossol

On the coast, north of Gustavia, Corossol is a fishing village that has maintained the early traditions. You'll enjoy seeing the Creole houses (*cases*), the older women wearing large white bonnets and modest dress, and visiting the stores that sell the handwoven straw items made here.

Colombier

A tiny residential community on the island's northern fork, Colombier has both traditional and modern homes, lovely gardens and a school. The views from the outskirts of Colombier take in all the offshore islands as well as most of St. Barts. Although it has no beach, you can hike to lovely beach areas from here.

 # Sights

La Grande Saline

The old salt flats used until the 1970s are now way stations for migrating birds.

Vitet

The highest mountain on St. Barts soars to 900 feet. The island astrologer owns a small inn here.

Geography

The islands of the Lesser Antilles are like tiny blips in a sea of blue. St. Martin and Anguilla are the most northerly islands and St. Barts is 20 miles (32 km) to the south. St. Barts is also much smaller, covering only eight square miles (25 square km). It has an irregular coastline which creates scores of coves and bays, many protected by coral reefs.

St. Barts does not have any freshwater lakes or rivers. Drinking water is collected in cisterns and saltwater is processed at the local desalinization plant. A rugged mountain range, which includes Vitet, the highest peak, forms the island's spine, creating stunning views.

All roads (paved only in the last 30 years) wind around and over the mountains. Narrow winding roads (also paved) lead from the main road to the coastline.

There is one major road with branches.

Climate

Temperatures are moderated by the trade winds, which cross the island from east to west. Carrying moisture from the Atlantic Ocean (the Atlantic meets the Caribbean off Turtle Island in Grand Cul de Sac), the winds meet resistance at the mountain range. As they rise, they drop their moisture in the form of rain, making the eastern portion of the island green, filled with lush tropical vegetation. This is the windward side (*côte au vent* in French). The western portion of the island gets far less rain and wind. Vegetation on the leeward side (*côte sous le vent*) is sparser, not as colorful, and includes cactus. The vast majority of the flowering plants and trees here have been planted and are tended by residents.

An imaginary line from St. Jean to Gouverneur divides the island into the windward and leeward sides.

Although there is no specific rainy season, St. Barts is in the hurricane belt. In September 1995 Hurricane Luis caused great damage to the vegetation, beaches and buildings.

★ DID YOU KNOW?

Fortunately, a heavy rain a few days after Hurricane Luis washed much of the salt off the vegetation, allowing it to rejuvenate quickly. Although some beaches lost sand, others were enlarged.

Flora & Fauna

Plant Life

On the windward (eastern) portion of the island, flowering plants grow wild by roadsides, in ravines and along hiking trails on the hills. You'll see pink, yellow and orange hibiscus, Mexican creepers, frangipani, bougainvillea, flamboyants, white lilies and even orchids. On the leeward (western) side you'll see less vegetation, but locals have done a magnificent job of planting and watering. As you explore the traditional towns of Colombier and Corossol you'll notice the flourishing gardens around the Creole houses.

Animal Life

There is no fresh water on St. Barts, so there are no indigenous animals. Mongooses and iguanas were introduced by settlers. Birds are the most interesting of the wildlife here. The brown pelican is so ubiquitous that it is one of the island's symbols. Watch it glide effortlessly above the sea and then plunge into the water at what seems like 100 mph to scoop up unsuspecting fish. You'll also see black frigate birds with white or red throats, kingfishers, herons, hummingbirds and tiny bananaquits.

In the waters around the island are spiny lobsters, dorados, sharks, yellowtail snappers, tuna, conch and whelks.

A Brief History

You're going on vacation. There's sea, sand and great food. Who cares about the island's history? Normally we would agree but, in the case of St. Barts, the island is so unusual that you'll definitely be curious. Although you may not read this section before you leave home, you will appreciate it after spending a day on the island. We promise to keep it short.

Discovered by Columbus on his second voyage (1493-1496), the island was named for his younger brother Bartholomew – St. Barthelemeo. Columbus moved on; with no fresh water and no people, the island was largely useless to him. Even the Carib Indians living on nearby islands stopped here only to fish.

The island was first noted on Spanish maps in 1523.

Although the Pope gave the whole New World to Spain in 1494, the Spanish did not consider these tiny islands of any importance and left them for France and Britain, who both established colonies on nearby St. Christopher (now St. Kitts). In 1634, Pierre d'Esnambuc (sponsored by the French on St. Kitts) landed on St. Barts and liked it. He set off for France to gather settlers. He returned to the area with about 500 people, mostly peasants from Normandy and Brittany. The majority chose to stay on St. Kitts, while others stayed on Guadeloupe and Martinique. Only about 60 arrived on St. Barts in 1648.

The governor of the French colonies, Longvilliers de Poincy, was also a commander in the Knights of Malta. This order was founded during the Crusades to aid soldiers and pilgrims en route to the Holy Land. As the Spanish became more prominent in the area, they menaced the small French colony. De Poincy sold St. Barts and the French side of St. Martin to the Knights, thereby gaining a protective force, while he continued to govern.

Unfortunately, the Knights did not recognize the threat from the Carib Indians. The Indians massacred the entire colony, which made it more difficult to attract new settlers. Yet, since it had an excellent harbor and a strategic position surrounded by British possessions, the governor of St. Kitts cajoled 100 hardy Huguenots from Normandy and Brittany to try again.

No Water, No Slaves

With no fresh water and little arable land, no plantations were established on St. Barts and there was no need for slaves. Unlike the majority of islands in the West Indies, there are very few black people living on the island. Those that do live here are descendants of workers from nearby islands who were recruited to labor in the shipyards.

St. Barts began to prosper because of its harbor. Pirates of all nationalities made the island their headquarters, bringing the treasures they had plundered from Spanish galleons, when having their ships repaired and restocked. One well-known cutthroat, Montbars the Exterminator (is that a great name!) made St. Barts his home.

Montbars the Exterminator

As a boy, the French-born Montbars had read of the cruelties of the Spanish as they conquered the New World. He vowed revenge, and was so successful that he earned the name "Exterminator." Montbars was lost at sea during a hurricane and never returned to excavate his loot. Legend has it buried near Anse de Gouverneur or Grande Saline on the south coast. Bring your shovels!

Although prospering, St. Barts was ceded by King Louis XVI to his friend King Gustaf III of Sweden in exchange for free-port rights in Gothenburg. In 1784, the Swedes, who had no other possessions in the New World, became rulers of St. Barts. They took their responsibility seriously. They laid out a grid of streets on both sides of the harbor, renaming the town (then called Carenage) for their King, Gustavia. They carved winding roads through the island, built a town hall, made the island a duty-free port (which it still is today) and constructed three forts. Forts Gustaf, Octave and Karl are still visible today, with Gustaf on the hill in town. Best of all, they did not impose their culture on the islanders, but rather permitted local traditions to continue.

Look for Swedish names on streets.

The island boomed and by 1800 there were over 6,000 residents. Unfortunately, as neighboring islands expanded their port facilities, trade moved north, especially to the Danish Virgin Islands (now US). Many St. Barthians left the island to form a community on St. Thomas. They called it Carenage, and it still exists today.

There are about 6,000 residents on St. Barts today as well.

Hurricanes and a huge fire in 1852 decimated Gustavia. It was not rebuilt. In 1967 only 400 people lived in Gustavia.

In 1878, after 92 years, the Swedes sold St. Barts back to France. It remains part of France today, with locals voting for the French President and Prime Minister. It is governed through Guadeloupe, but elects a local mayor and municipal council.

St. Barts remains an anachronism. Older residents cling to the centuries-old traditions of their native Breton, Norman and Swedish ancestors, while the younger are moving rapidly into the world of rock music, Sunday football games and cheeseburgers.

Sunup To Sundown

Since St. Barts' weather is near-perfect year-round, you'll spend many of your daylight hours on the beaches, either on a lounge chair working on your tan or enjoying watersports. But the island has over 20 distinct beaches and the coves and bays that house them are on all parts of the island. Virtually every town and village was established near a beach or marina, so you'll be sightseeing as you head to a new beach. Swimming beaches have thick white sand and calm waters. Several have coral reefs that even a beginner can snorkel over, while others are perfect for windsurfing, boardsurfing, spearfishing or shell-collecting.

Beach areas that do not have a hotel are undeveloped. There are no lounge chairs, umbrellas or food. Bring a blanket, find a seagrape tree and bring a picnic lunch. Most of the beach areas are easily accessed by car. You may have a short walk across the dunes from the parking lot. In just a few cases, the walk is a true hike, as in Colombier; others are reached only by boat. Often, these boat-accessed beaches are popular with local scuba operators.

Topless bathing is the norm on St. Barts, both on beaches and at poolside. Although nude bathing is officially illegal, nobody pays much attention to it and it is commonplace on isolated beaches on the island's rugged southern shore.

> **◉ TIP**
>
> All beaches are open to the public, even those that front a hotel. Non-hotel guests can rent watersports gear, eat at the hotel's restaurant, and use the pool for a fee.

You can play tennis or squash, then go horseback riding or bicycling.

Your beach-hopping and island exploring will depend on what activities you enjoy most, but we'll start with Gustavia, the delightful capital. It is the only place on the island you simply must see. You can easily explore the downtown commercial area on foot.

Gustavia & Shell Beach

St. Barts is the only island in the Caribbean that has Sweden as part of its heritage. In this capital (which was named for the Swedish king Gustav) you'll find that the streets have both Swedish and French names. When you shop, you'll sing the praises of good King Gustav, who declared this town a duty-free port, a status it still holds today. Gustavia's beautiful harbor is often dotted with luxury yachts and sailboats tied to its berths. In the distance at the harbor's entrance, you might notice a cruise ship at anchor. The passengers are ferried ashore in dinghies. Don't be alarmed by the onslaught of tourists: the locals, determined not to be over-run by cruise passengers, limit the number of ships.

The town has two legs (on either side of the har-bor); the far side is called **La Pointe**. It has an old Swedish fort, the newly renovated **Wall House Museum and Library**, and scores of restaurants, but all the action is on the near-side. It has many restaurants, as well as the shops, historic buildings and an open-air mar-ket, **Le Ti Marché**, which is fun to explore.

There are very few buildings of historic interest left in town because of the damage wrought by a hurricane and then a fire in 1852. The oldest building in town is the **Vieux Clocher**, on rue du Presbitaire. This bell tower, built in 1799, once sat adjacent to a church that no longer exists. The bell, which rang to mark special events, has been replaced by a clock.

The **Mairie**, now the town hall, was formerly called the Governor's House and used to be the home of Swedish governors. It retains the Swedish architectural style with its green and white façade and stone foundation. It's on rue Auguste Nyman, which is the continuation of rue de Roi Oscar II.

St. Barts

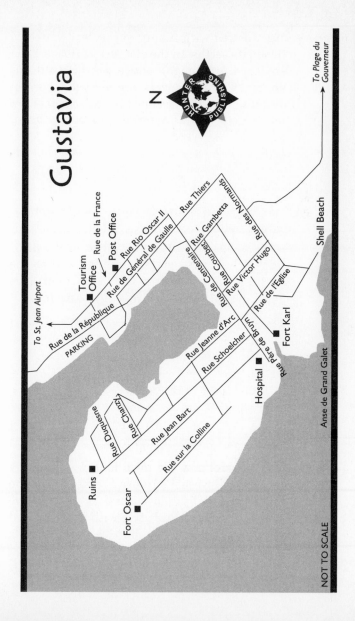

Gustavia

N

To St. Jean Airport

Tourism
Office

Rue de la France

Post Office

Rue Rio Oscar II

Rue de Général de Gaulle

Rue Thiers

Rue de la République

PARKING

Rue Gambetta

Rue Centenaire

Rue Coubertin

Rue des Normands

Rue Victor Hugo

Rue de l'Eglise

To Plage du Gouverneur

Shell Beach

Rue Jeanne d'Arc

Rue Schoelcher

Rue Père de Bruyn

Fort Karl

Hospital

Rue Duquesne

Rue Chanzy

Rue Jean Bart

Rue sur la Colline

Ruins

Fort Oscar

Anse de Grand Galet

NOT TO SCALE

Two 19th-century churches, both of which which still hold services, are on the streets just above the harbor. The **Catholic Church** on rue du Presbitaire (near the old clock tower) was built in 1822. It is similar to the one in Lorient, which was the island's first Catholic church. It has whitewashed walls and a lovely garden. Note the separate bell tower that is taller than the church, allowing the chimes to be heard everywhere.

The **Anglican Church** is on rue de Centenaire, a major street that joins both legs of the harbor and houses the post office. The church is starting to show its age and is quite weathered.

★ DID YOU KNOW?

The dark stones on the corners of the Anglican church were brought from St. Eustatius, while the stones of the façade and steps were brought from France.

Nearby, the "Place de la Retrocession" (formerly Place du Bicentenaire) was dedicated in August 2000 to commemorate the return of the island to France after 93 years of Swedish rule. Look for the huge anchor, which was dredged from the harbor. It probably came from an American warship that was in use between 1700 and 1825.

The Swedes built three defensive forts around the harbor. **Fort Oscar** still guards the entrance at La Pointe, although it is closed to the public. **Fort Gustav**, at the entrance to town (near Public Beach) may be visited but isn't too exciting. **Fort Karl** is only a memory.

The **Municipal Museum & Library** is often called The Wall House Museum because it is situated in an old Swedish warehouse of that name. The building is on rue Schoelcher at the farthest point of La Pointe. The front is marked by cannons and Swedish and French flags. The inner building was badly damaged by the 1852 fire but, fortunately, the façade remains solid. Both the museum and library offer a journey back through time to discover the island's roots. There are texts, historical engravings and maps that trace the island from the times of Columbus to the Knights of Malta, Montbars the Exterminator and the Swedes. Documents, watercolors, and portraits abound. It's small but very interesting. Hours are Monday-Friday, 8:30 am to 12:30 and 2:30 to 6 pm. Saturdays it's open from 9 to 11 am. Closed Sunday. Small fee.

Two interesting spots are beyond the "downtown" area. The first is **Anse de Grand Calet**, better known as Shell Beach, which is just a five-minute walk from town. Dredging of the harbor in 1960 revealed the shells that continue to wash onto the shore here.

This is not a great swimming beach.

The other point of interest, at Public Beach on the way into town (look for the desalinization plant), is the old **Swedish cemetery**, which has some weathered stones dating from the 18th century. A stone memorial to Swedes who stayed on after the island was returned to France was placed here by Sweden's king when he visited in 1978.

Having exhausted the town's historical sites, you have two choices – lunch or shopping. Look for lunch suggestions under *Lunch at the Beach*, page 107.

Saint Jean & Saint Jean Beach

At the heart of the island, this is the closest thing to "bustling" that you'll find on St. Barts. There is always something going on in the tiny village, whether it is a plane taking off or landing, people shopping at the small in-town shopping centers, or families swimming, windsurfing or jogging along the island's most popular beach strip.

Great views here of the airport and all of St. Jean.

It's always fun watching the planes, like giant birds, as they swoop over the mountain and immediately drop to the runway. You can't stand at the end of the runway (which stops at the shore), so people head to the top of the mountain, which locals have humorously named La Tourmente (The Torment).

Two **shopping centers** are directly across the roadway from the terminal. The **Galeries du**

Commerce Saint Jean and **La Savane Centre Commercial** have shops that serve both locals and tourists. The **Match** supermarket dominates La Savane. Terrific for those renting villas, it has fresh meats, fish and produce, as well as canned foods from France and the US. Hours are 8 am-1 pm and 3-8 pm, Monday-Thursday; Friday and Saturday, 8 am-10 pm; and Sunday, 9 am-1 pm and 4-7 pm. Look for **Maya's To Go** next door. A gourmet take-out shop, it offers a daily sandwich menu as well as meats, fish and salads for take-out. Wines and soft drinks as well. Other shops include **Tropic Video**, a beauty salon, sunglass and clothing boutiques and a music store.

The Eden Rock Hotel juts out into the bay, effectively breaking the beach into two distinct strips. The strip between the Eden Rock and Lorient has been greatly built up with several shopping areas. Small **Le Pelican Plage** houses only a few shops, but they include an antiquarian book and map store and an art gallery. The informal **Pelican Restaurant** serves lunch and dinner.

Across the road, **La Presse** is your best bet for English-language reading materials. It faces **Ki Ki-e Mo**, a small café and Italian gourmet take-out shop.

Soon you'll see St. Barts' largest shopping center, **La Villa Créole**. It houses several branch shops of boutiques in Gustavia and cigar, handicraft and perfume shops as well. **La Créole**

Restaurant, the island's only brasserie, serves from 7 am till 11 pm daily. It's easier to park at **Centre Vavel** across Salines Road. Here you'll find **La Rotisserie**, a popular take-out shop and a host of other stores, including a pharmacy.

Saint Jean Beach is the most popular beach on the island for local families, flirting teenagers and the young people who work at the shops and hotels. The bay is very long and the wide strip is covered with thick white sand. There are several watersports centers renting snorkel gear, surfboards, windsurfers and other items. They also give lessons. This is a great swimming beach with a natural coral reef. Saint Jean Beach fronts many of the hotels we've detailed and a few others are on the hillsides nearby. There are good restaurants too. The area behind the beach is also residential, with villa communities and individually owned villas overlooking the sea.

Remember that topless bathing is the norm at beaches and pools on the island.

At Saint Jean, the main road continues eastward to Lorient (we will follow it), and there is a branch road leading inland over the mountains to the southern shore.

Lorient
(Anse de Lorient)

Lorient, the site of the first French settlement on St. Barts, is a picturesque village that sits on the crossroads of the main road with the road inland to Vitet and the southern coast. The 19th-century **Catholic church** here has been restored. Similar to the one in Gustavia, the bell tower is adjacent to it. Also in town are two **French cemeteries** that are striking because they are so immaculate. The tombs are slightly raised, with crosses marking each headstone. Atop each freshly painted white tomb you'll see lighted red candles and flowers – some fresh and some plastic. On November 1st and 2nd, locals observe All Soul's and All Saint's Day, two traditional Catholic holidays. On those days there are candlelight processions to the cemeteries and the local parish priest leads the marchers in prayer.

Here too you'll find **Le Manoir,** a Norman manor that was built in the early 1600s. It was shipped from France and reconstructed here in 1984 by a French artist. Now a B&B (see *Best Places to Stay*, page 79), it has a wonderful garden with a waterfall and lily pond. The "M" line of local fragrances and lotions developed here are sold as well. You'll also find a gas station, post office, two mini-markets, several small hotels and an elementary school, where the children are often at play in the yard.

Anse de Lorient Beach is extremely long, and, except for Sundays when many local families head there, it is very quiet. While most of the beach has calm waters, the far end has pounding waves that are prime surfing waters, especially in winter. You'll see lots of young people testing the waves.

▣ TIP

The "Reefer Surf Club," an informal group, meets at Anse de Lorient Beach. They offer surfing advice to beginners and experienced surfers.

Pointe Milou

Pointe Milou does not have a beach, but surfers congregate on the rocky shore because the waves are terrific. It is a beautiful area and many of St. Barts' loveliest residences are here.

★ DID YOU KNOW?

Rockefellers, Fords, well-known dancers and rock stars have homes above the bay.

Anse Marigot & Grand Cul de Sac Beach

The road starts to climb as it approaches Marigot Bay, which is a popular area for sailing and swimming. At the peak of the hill, you'll see the stunning bay of Grand Cul de Sac. Three of the island's best hotels are on its shores. The Atlantic Ocean meets the Caribbean Sea at Turtle Island here. The bay is quite calm, with coral reefs for snorkelers. There are three active watersports centers here. The one at St. Barth Beach Hotel has a respected windsurfing school. You can windsurf, waterski or sail through these waters. The beach is shaded by trees and is the second most popular after Saint Jean.

There are no towns in this area.

Anse Petit Cul-De-Sac, Anse Toiny & Grand Frond

These coves mark the start of the island's undeveloped and rugged southern shore. The coast is lined by sheer rock cliffs and there is no sand. Boulders near the shore prohibit swimming, but the area does offer beautiful views and the freshest air on the island.

⚡ WARNING

Some intrepid surfers chal-
lenge the waves at Toiny, but
we don't recommend it.

*A few hardy
surfers try their
skills here too.*

At Petit Cul de Sac you can see natural caves in
the rock walls. Nearby you'll spot the local joke
called the **"Washing Machine,"** where seawa-
ter runs into a natural rock pool and swirls
around, creating foam.

★ DID YOU KNOW?

Rocks from Petit Cul de Sac
were used to build the church in
Lorient.

You can follow the footpath from Anse Toiny
(near the posh hotel) to Anse Grand Frond. En
route you'll pass a typical St. Barts cottage
called the **Cabrette**, which was built of stone
and withstood even Hurricane Luis. You'll also
go by a private chapel built by a family in memory of a loved one. (There are others in Vitet,
Saline and Corossol.)

Grande Saline
(Anse de Grande
Saline)

On the way to Grande Saline, the road drops to
sea level and follows the rugged coast with an
occasional wave washing over the road.

> **▣ TIP**
>
> Notice the dry rock walls along the Morne Vitet (mountain), which look like the walls on Ireland's Aran Islands.

This part of St. Barts is exciting because it is so undeveloped and wide open. The two cloudy patches you see are the former salt ponds (salines) from which salt was extracted until the 1970s. They look ghostly, especially now that they are enveloped by mangroves with wild vegetation. These salt ponds have become a way station for migrating birds.

Stay left at the crossroads or you will be on your way back to Lorient.

Grande Saline Beach is arguably the most stunning beach on the island. Park in the area provided and walk over the dunes to the pristine beach. As far as the eye can see there is only thick white sand and sparkling blue water.

Le Grain de Sel Restaurant, page 106, is adjacent to the parking lot.

> **▣ TIP**
>
> There are no facilities on the beach so bring a blanket, food and water, and enjoy. This beach is so isolated that it is very popular with nude bathers.

Lurin & Anse du Gouverneur

Waves here are great for surfing and swimming.

The area near the town of Lurin, which is residential, resembles areas of rural France, complete with small houses and pretty gardens. The parking lot here is near a private house. Follow the path to the beach, which vies with Grande Saline for the top prize. Shaded by seagrape trees, the sand stretches for over half a mile. The far point, called Grande Pointe, is where the pirate Montbars was supposed to have buried his treasure.

▣ TIP

There are no facilities. Head to nearby Santa Fe Café or bring picnic fixings.

Corossol (Anse de Corossol)

Corossol is a small fishing village in the northwest part of the island. It is of little interest to visitors except for the fact that it is the most traditional village on St. Barts. It offers a glimpse of life in rural Normandy and Brittany long ago. Many of the residents speak to one another in an old Norman dialect (they speak French, too), and some of the older women dress in modest skirts and shoulder-length white bonnets called *quicheonettes*. Many of them own or work in the handicraft shops that dot the town. The items sold here are woven using the fronds of latania trees from nearby Anse des Flamands, which were introduced to the island by a French priest. He taught local women how to weave the palms, which they did while their husbands were at sea. They make Panama hats, wicker baskets, place mats and bags.

Cases (Traditional Houses)

Corossol also has many traditional St. Barts houses called *cases*. Built to withstand the elements, they sit on a rock base, with the lumber sunk into concrete. The houses are low to the ground and all the doors and windows face west (less wind). The red roof is four-sided and bordered by gutters that trap the rain and direct it to cisterns. The houses are painted in contrasting pastels. They are small and entire families live in one or two rooms. Hammocks are popular and take up less space than beds. The kitchen is in an adjoining building. This avoids the risk of fire and keeps the house cooler. The houses are surrounded by gardens.

The beach at Anse de Corossol is filled with fishing boats and is not one of the best beaches for swimming.

> 🔲 **TIP**
>
> Visit the **Inter-Oceans Museum** in Corossol if you like seashells. It has 7,000.

Anse des Cayes & Anse des Flamands

These two bays are adjacent to one another on the island's northern coast, but intervening rock cliffs make it necessary to return to the main road and take a branch road to each.

Anse des Cayes, the smaller of the two, is dominated by the deluxe Manapany Cottages. The rest of the cove is residential, with beautiful villas on the hills that encircle the bay. It's hard to believe when you are driving here, but Anse des Cayes is the cove just west of Saint Jean. If you follow the worn path up the hill you'll be overlooking the airport and town. This bay is very popular with surfers because it is unprotected on both sides. Spearfishermen seem to have success at the western end and a few walk-in scuba divers have fun not too far from shore.

The waters here are calm and perfect for swimming, snorkeling, and windsurfing.

> 🔲 **TIP**
>
> **Chez Ginette**, owned by a vivacious islander, is a good spot to sample a refreshing coconut punch on Anse des Cayes.

Anse des Flamands fronts a tiny village of about 300 residents who live in the stunning villas overlooking the beach. Many of the villas are rented out for part of the year. The hills are alive with banana and coconut palms as well as hibiscus, bouganvillea and lilies. The thick white sand strip is so long that the Isle de France Hotel (see page 59) occupies only a tiny portion of it. Shaded by seagrape trees and latania palms, the strip attracts many joggers at dusk.

You can eat in the beach-side restaurant at the Isle de France and use the pool.

Paths lead from the beach to the top of the volcano (now extinct) that gave birth to St. Barts long ago. Even more interesting is the rocky winding path that leads to Colombier Beach (about a 25-minute walk – you'll need closed shoes).

If you follow the beach road past Anse des Flamands you'll find a tiny beach, La Petite Anse. There's not much sand but there is great snorkeling. Anse des Flamands is every bit as lovely as Grande Saline and Gouverneur.

Colombier & Colombier Beach

Unlike its neighbor Corossol, the town of Colombier at the island's northwest tip is quite modern. You'll pass a church, a school and homes, as well as many neighborhood shops. As the road enters town, you'll be struck by the awesome views (this part of the island is well above sea level). Its western location assures you that the sunsets are unrivaled, and there are many lookout points in town where you can stop. The best one is near the "Orientation Map," which is carved in stone. It pinpoints all the sights, which include most of St. Barts, the small islands offshore, St. Martin, and, on a really clear day, Anguilla.

Colombier Beach offers good swimming and snorkeling.

Colombier Beach is stunning and totally pristine, but it is far below the town. To reach it you can follow the trail from the end of town. It's downhill, but remember that you'll have to climb back up. Give yourself 20 minutes going down and at least 10 more (i.e., 30 minutes) coming back. You'll find the trail rocky and the vegetation, which includes cactus, quite dry. Since it is easily reached by boat, the beach is filled with sailboats and motorboats.

Hike to Colombier Beach from Anse des Flamands (see above).

> 🔲 **TIP**
>
> Readers have written to say that the hike back up to the town is quite taxing in the heat. Don't forget to bring water, as none is available here.

Land-Based Sports

Tennis & Squash

Courts can be lit for night play. Hotel guests get preference.

Guanahani Hotel, ☎ 590-27-66-60, two tennis courts.

Isle de France Hotel, ☎ 590-27-61-81. One tennis and one a/c squash court.

Your concierge can help you with arrangements.

Manapany Cottages, ☎ 590-27-66-55. One tennis court.

St. Barths Beach Hotel, ☎ 590-27-62-63. One tennis court.

Le Flamboyant Tennis Club, ☎ 590-27-69-82. Two tennis courts.

Reefer Surf Club, ☎ 590-27-67-63. One squash court.

Horseback Riding

Ranch des Flamands (Anse des Flamands) has two-hour rides for beginners and experienced riders. Excursions leave at 9 am and 3 pm. ☎ 590-27-80-72.

Golf

Molokai Golf Club (Grand Cul de Sac) has a driving range. There is no golf course on the island. ☎ 590-37-46-45.

Hiking

You can hike on St. Barts but there are only a few marked trails. A beautiful one connects Anse des Flamands and Colombier Beach and a steeper one connects Marigot Bay and Morne Vitet. Check at the tourist office for trail maps and suggestions.

Bicycle Rentals

St. Barts is quite mountainous. Be prepared for lots of ups and downs. You can bike on the roads and on more rugged terrain. Get details when you rent. All of the places listed here are in Gustavia.

Rent Some Fun (mountain bikes)
. . . . ☎ 590-27-70-59
Ounalao . . . . ☎ 590-27-81-27
Ernest Ledee . . . . ☎ 590-27-61-63

Spa Services & Fitness Centers

The Eden Rock Hotel Spa (St. Jean) is the most elegant on the island. It offers beauty treatments and massages. Open to the public. ☎ 590-29-79-99.

Salines Massages (Salines) is another good choice. Their French-trained staff gives massages, facials, waxing and nail care. ☎ 590-29-76-75.

Blue Agency of Beauty sends licensed professionals to your hotel or villa for hair and skin care, massages and nail treatments. ☎ 590-29-74-22.

St. Barth Gym (Cul de Sac) is a well-equipped gym with cardiovascular machines, weights and step boards. Classes are held and private instruction is offered. ☎ 590-67-24-08. Similar, **Forma Form** is in Gustavia. ☎ 590-27-51-23.

Water-Based Sports

Snorkeling

You can rent gear at every waterfront center. If you want to buy some, head to **Loulou's Marine** on Gustavia's dock. ☎ 590-27-62-74.

Scuba Trips

A variety of scuba trips are organized by certified operators. There are many dive sites near the island, particularly off its western coast. Single- and double-tank dives, night dives, wrecks, deep dives and dives for children are all available. Equipment is provided. Half-day and full-day trips are offered.

It's a good idea to make plans before your arrival.

West Indies Dives. . . . . . ☎ 590-27-70-34
Yacht Club Dock, Gustavia

Mermaid Diving Center . . ☎ 590-58-79-29
(cell) Grand Cul de Sac, El Sereno Hotel

La Bulle Diving Ctr. . . . . ☎ 590-27-62-25
Gustavia

St. Barth Plongée, Gustavia ☎ 590-27-54-44

Odyssée Caraïbe, La Pointe ☎ 590-27-55-94

Windsurfing & Sailing

Windsurfing is the most popular watersport here. There are all levels of instruction and the finest equipment. St. Jean, Grand Cul de Sac and Anse des Cayes are the best sites.

Wind Wave Power . . . . . ☎ 590-27-62-57
St. Barths Beach Hotel, Grand Cul de Sac

Eden Rock Sea Sport Club ☎ 590-29-79-93
Eden Rock Hotel, St. Jean

Reefer Surf Club . . . . . . ☎ 590-22-67-63
Lorient Beach

St. Barth Waterplay Bic Center
Saint Jean Beach. . . . . . . ☎ 590-27-71-22

Jet Skiing

F.W.I. Watersport . . . . . ☎ 590-27-52-06
Yacht Club Dock, Gustavia

Wind Wave Power . . . . . ☎ 590-27-82-57
St. Barth Beach Hotel, Grand Cul de Sac

Master Ski Pilou . . . . . . ☎ 590-27-91-79
Gustavia

Eden Rock Sea Sport Club
Eden Rock Hotel, St. Jean . . ☎ 590-27-74-77

Daytrips & Deep-Sea Fishing

Marine Service . . . . ☎ 590-27-70-34
Yacht Club Dock, Gustavia

Ocean Must . . . . ☎ 590-27-62-25
La Pointe (near Wall House), Gustavia

St. Barth Plongée . . . . . ☎ 590-27-54-44
Quai de la République, Gustavia

Master Ski Pilou . . . . . . ☎ 590-27-91-79
Gustavia

*These are the
largest water-
sports centers on
St. Barts.*

These companies offer the widest range of watersports activities. They organize daily half- and full-day snorkel trips to secluded bays and uninhabited cays. Gear, instruction and refreshments are included.

Each has crewed charter-fishing boats with IGFA-approved equipment. Trips include shore fishing, as well as deep-sea fishing. For groups of four or more.

▣ TIP

Fishing is best between April and September, but there is fishing year-round. Catches include tuna, bonito, dorado, marlin, wahoo and barracuda.

Yacht Charters & Motorboat Rentals

Nautica FWI, rue de la République. ☎ 590-27-56-50. Represents deluxe crewed yachts (one-week minimum).

Poupon Marine, rue du Roi Oscar. ☎ 590-27-79-36. Crewed and uncrewed yachts for use by the week or longer.

St. Barth Caraïbes Yachting. ☎ 590-27-52-06. Motorboats.

Yannis Marine. ☎ 590-29-89-12. Rents motorboats and organizes day-trips.

Marine Service. ☎ 590-27-70-34. Motorboats and sailboats.

Surfboards & Snorkel Gear

Waterplay, Bic Center, Saint Jean
. . . . ☎ 590-27-71-22

Hookipa Surf Shop, Saint Jean (rentals)
. . . . ☎ 590-27-71-31

Hookipa Surf Shop, Gustavia (sales)
. . . . ☎ 590-27-76-57

West Indian Surf Shop . . ☎ 590-27-90-01
Salinas Road in Saint Jean (rentals and sales)

Loulou's Marine, Gustavia (sales)
. . . . ☎ 590-27-62-74

Waterskiing

St. Barth Caraïbes Yachting
. . . . ☎ 590-27-52-48
Marine Service . . . . ☎ 590-27-70-34
Ocean Must . . . . ☎ 590-27-62-25

The Marine Nature Reserve of St. Barths

Local and national authorities became involved in the movement to protect St. Barts' rich marine legacy by establishing the Marine Nature Reserve in 1996. It is situated on the northern and western parts of the island and encompasses 2,965 acres. The goal is to preserve the coral reefs, seagrass beds and the marine life in the reserve.

There are 43 coral species in the reserve as well as ascidies, sea sponges and anemones. They provide shelter for sea urchins, starfish, shellfish and crustaceans, as well as 165 species of fish. Some sea turtles are found here as well. There are five distinct zones – in some, light fishing, diving and watersports are allowed, while in others only scientific research is permitted.

The best way to visit the reserve is to take a sailing or snorkeling trip (only sailboats are allowed). These include half-day, full-day or sunset sails. Gear, snacks and open bar are included. Lunch is served on the full-day trip. Call Marine Service, ☎ 590-27-70-34, for reservations.

Shop Till You Drop

There are dozens of boutiques in downtown Gustavia. You can't miss them as you stroll along rue Charles de Gaulle and Quai de la République, which also has a mall. New shops have opened on rue du Bord de Mer (at dockside) and along rue de la France as well.

You should also explore the shops at St. Jean's shopping areas. Villa Créole, the largest, has lured some independent names, as well as branch stores of downtown boutiques. Centre Vaval and Le Plage Pelican nearby make this trio, between Eden Rock Hotel and Lorient, a commercial hub. Smaller, but with a few upscale shops, are the Galeries du Commerce, St. Jean and La Savanne, across from the airport.

Shops sell imported fashions from France and Italy for both men and women, jewelry, watches, leather goods and shoes, fine perfumes, cigars, wines and liquors and local arts and crafts.

St. Barts

> **▣ TIP**
>
> St. Barts is a duty-free port. This means that the imported sportswear and leather goods are less expensive than they would be in Paris or Milan, but don't expect bargains.

Store Hours

Weekdays, shops open at 9 am (a few open at 8). At 12 noon (or 12:30) the doors are locked, the gates are pulled down, and shop owners and salespersons head to lunch. They re-open at 2:30 pm until 7. On Saturday, stores open from 9 am to 12:30 pm and most do not re-open in the afternoon. Stores are closed on Sundays.

Gustavia Boutiques

Most of the designer boutiques are in **Le Carré d'Or**, a multi-level mall that looks like a mini-version of Los Angeles' Rodeo Drive. It is on the Quai de la République opposite the harbor. **Hermès** and **Cartier** stand at the entrance and you'll find **Polo**, **Versace**, and **Stephane and Bernard**, a local shop that sells imported designer fashions, such as Ungaro, Valentino and Hervé Leger. **The Ventura Shop's** designer lines include Fendi, Céline and Pucci. **Oro del Sol**, an upscale jeweler, has a shop

Most shops accept major credit cards, travelers' checks and US dollars.

here, as does **Chopard Jewelers**. **Lolita** and **What's Up?** sell bikinis and active sportswear, while **Metis** sells shoes and handbags. **Privilège** sells perfumes and lotions. There are any number of interesting shops to rummage through.

Rue de France & Rue Charles de Gaulle

Look for **Passage de la Crémaillère** on rue Charles de Gaulle. The shops in this new bi-level arcade feature sportswear and resortwear, as well as designer fashions.

Blanc Bleu, **St. Barths French West Indies** and **Lunette Sunglasses** offer items for young fashionistas.

Elysées Caraïbes sells Lancel luggage and Longchamp leathers.

Human Steps sells high-fashion shoes and boots for men and women, including Prada and Charles Jourdan.

Hugo Boss has its own boutique on rue Charles de Gaulle.

Marc Segre sells Burberry leather goods and fashions.

Appunto sells Donna Karan, Moschino, Versace and D&G for ladies and men.

Peer sells upscale T-shirts and activewear.

Mi Bolo offers locally made pottery and spices.

Laurant Effel has fine leather shoes, handbags and belts for both sexes. High-style, most items are from Paris.

La Comptoir des Antilles sells English language newspapers and magazines.

Le Comptoir de Cigare has a selection of the world's best cigars and is the most attractive shop here. Step into the humidor room and select from Dunhill, Davidoff, Dominican and Jamaican brands as well as best-sellers from Cuba. They sell humidors and Panama hats as well.

Remember that Cuban cigars cannot be brought back into the US.

Goldfinger has shops on every Caribbean island, including St. Barts. An attractive shop selling fine watches, jewelry, crystal and perfumes.

Carat nearby has Christofle pieces as well as Piaget watches, while its neighbor **Kornerupine** sells 18K gold jewelry from Charmet of Paris, Breitling and Jaeger Le Coultre watches and the very hot Ingénieur chrome alarm watch.

Nomades is an eclectic shop with attractively priced sundresses, pareos, strawbags and T-shirts.

Two great stops for T-shirts and the like are **Outremer** and **Loulou's Marine**. Outremer sells shorts, cotton tote bags and straw items. Loulou's, a chandler's shop, sells the white and olive green totebags with their name and logo that are very fashionable here.

Blue Coast, a shop that specializes in linen clothing, is adjacent to the **La Coste Store** on rue du Bord de Mer. Here too you'll find **Manuel Canovas**, selling bathing suits, and **Optical Caraïbes**, for sunglasses

Le Goût du Vin is another attractive shop selling French wines and champagne (you'll recognize the names).

Pottery is a local handicraft using the traditional method of throwing clay on the wheel, forming it by hand, then glazing and firing it. Not only are the vases and pots beautifully painted, they are oven-safe. **St. Barts Pottery**, on La Pointe, has a large selection.

St. Jean Boutiques

The best shops are in the **Villa Créole**. Look for **Black Swan** that sells lingerie, **Boutique Ilena** that sells beachwear and **Made in St. Barth**, a boutique selling perfumes, lotion and soaps made on the island. Local art is sold as well. **Kiwi** sells beachwear for teens and young adults.

St. Barts Artists

There are many local artists and sculptors whose work is for sale at their individual galleries and at art galleries around the island. The **Municipal Tourist Office** (at the dock) has a list of artists and galleries. They will tell you which artists are in residence when you are visiting St. Barts and what kind of work they do.

Best Places to Stay

From the air St. Barts resembles a centipede, its irregular coastline creating *anses* (coves), *baies* (bays) and cul-de-sacs isolated from one another by the mountain range that threads through the heart of the island. Virtually all house beach strips and small exceptional hotels are reached by winding paved roads that drop vertically to the sea. Other hotels and most rental villas perch at irregular levels on the green hills that overlook the coast, and there is even a deluxe hotel in the capital, Gustavia.

The island has over 40 hotels and a small number of guest houses. While they vary widely in décor and ambience, they share certain char-

acteristics. Hotels are very small (the largest
has only 76 rooms). Some of the island's finest
stops have fewer than 20 rooms. No more than
a total of 600 rooms are available at any one
time.

In 1995, Hurricane Luis not only decimated St.
Martin, but swept through St. Barts as well.
Although damage here was not as extensive, it
did force renovations to rooms and restaurants
at several hotels. You will reap the benefits of
those face lifts.

Hotels are locally owned and often family managed, and only one hotel is part of an international chain. The owners and staff get to know
every guest. They pride themselves on their
European ambience. Deluxe choices have kitchenettes. Some hotels even allow pets, and most
offer shuttle service to and from the airport,
and include breakfast in the rate. Some offer
car rentals.

There are no high-rise hotels, so your accommodations will likely be a private cottage or in a
two-story unit. Invariably you'll be two steps
from the beach; you'll have a private terrace or
patio encircled by seagrape trees. Many accommodation choices have restaurants, some of
which are gourmet, drawing diners from other
parts of the island.

St. Barts' deluxe hotels are exceptional. They
are elegantly furnished and often have private
pools or Jacuzzis. They have tennis courts, fitness centers, satellite TV, in-room fax and exer-

cise bikes and serve breakfast on a private terrace. There are few inexpensive stops here, although we have ferreted out a bed & breakfast and several inns.

Because of the paucity of hotel rooms, a popular alternative is to rent a villa – a home away from home. Once again, options and prices vary from comfortable one-bedroom retreats to lavish multi-bedroom havens complete with swimming pool and jeep. Villas come with daily maid service. Several villa communities have been built by hotels either on-property or nearby. Villa guests have full hotel privileges. Other villas are individually owned. Rentals are handled by agencies both on the island and abroad.

Things to Consider

Rate Schedules

Hotels have several rates for different times of year. Some have as many as six, but the highest rates are in effect during the period from December 15 to the New Year's weekend. Hotels and villas often require a minimum stay during this period. High-season rates are in effect from early January through the end of April and again from November 1 through December 14. Rates are as much as 40% higher than in the off-season.

Off-Season Travel

One drawback to off-season is that many hotels (restaurants too) close for periods of time, with June, September and October being the most common. There is no routine to these closing times, but if your first choice is closed, your second is likely to be open.

> **★ TIP**
>
> Off-season is quite long, running from May through October. You can save a lot of money by visiting during this time.

Advance Bookings

Make reservations well in advance and make sure you pin down the things that are important to you, ensuring that all your needs will be met. Hotels, even small ones, have a variety of accommodations.

Alive Price Scale

Rates on the island are very high, reflecting the limited number of rooms. You are paying not just for your room but for the singular quality of the island. While most hotels quote rates in US dollars, some use euros. Credit cards are readily accepted, although a few smaller stops may require a cash (check) deposit.

Hotels have a wide variety of accommodations. Few fit neatly into our categories of Deluxe, Expensive, Moderate, Inexpensive, and most fit into several categories. The price ranges shown here are designed to give you a heads-up about hotel rates, but always check with the hotel itself.

Rates are based on a double room, per night in high season.

Deluxe. . . . . over US $600

Expensive . . . . US $300-$600

Moderate . . . . US $200-$299

Inexpensive . . . . under US $200

The Best Hotels

Guanahani Hotel
Box 109, Grand Cul de Sac
St. Barts, FWI 97098
☎ 590-27-66-60; fax 590-27-70-70;
www.guanahani-hotel.com
Expensive-Deluxe

Guanahani would be a small luxury resort on any island but St. Barts. Here it is huge. It has 72 rooms, spreads over seven acres, and is fronted by two beaches. A member of The Leading Hotels of the World, Guanahani has "it," but doesn't flaunt it. Everything is understated, using a mélange of pastel shades, tropical woods and Creole furniture to create a relaxed environment.

You can also reach them through Leading Hotels of the World, ☎ 800-223-6800.

Closed Sept.

It is a village of cottages, 40 in all, done in West Indies style, with high pitched roofs and tiled terraces. Accommodations vary, however, in size, décor and, perhaps most importantly, location. There are cottages near the beach, others near the pools, and still more by the tennis courts.

> ### ▣ TIP
>
> If you like to sleep in, you might not want to be near these facilities, so be sure to check when you make your reservation.

The newest cottages, all suites, sit on a hillside at the edge of the property overlooking a coconut plantation and villa owned by the Rothschild family. These are very modern, with polished wood floors, darker wood furniture, deeper pastels on the walls, sunken sitting areas and handcarved cabinets for the TVs, mini-bars and desks. A curved wall separates the living and sleeping areas. Bathrooms have marble showers (no tubs). Each has a private pool or Jacuzzi.

The original cottages are set throughout the property, with six facing the beach. Some have double rooms and others have suites. These units are more traditionally furnished than the newer ones, but still offer stocked mini-bars, satellite TVs, air-conditioning and terraces.

Guanahani's main building is a lovely Colonial-style house with a wrap-around terrace. It has a very large lobby that is casually divided into conversation areas. Some guests congregate at the piano, others at the bar or around the comfortable couches.

There are two beaches; two pools, each with lounge chairs and tables; a well-organized watersports center with snorkel gear, windsurfers and Jet Skis; two floodlit tennis courts; a fitness center; beauty salon; and boutiques.

L'Indigo is an informal restaurant at poolside, while Le Bartolomeo, a gourmet continental choice, is nearby. Each has theme dinners and after-dinner shows several nights a week.

When you pull over at the scenic stop near Marigot Bay and see Guanahani, you realize just how lovely it is.

St. Barth Isle de France Hotel

Box 612, Baie des Flamands
St. Barts, FWI 97098
☎ 590-27-61-81; fax 590-27-86-83;
www.isle-de-france.com
Expensive-Deluxe

Closed Sept.

A personal favorite tucked away in a forest of palm trees on breathtaking Flamands Beach, the Isle de France was built in 1992. Although the hotel was renovated after Hurricane Luis, new owners have redecorated and added new facilities. The results are stunning – informal, yet elegant.

The main building, a two-story replica of a Colonial-era plantation house, is a happy blend of old-world-style and new facilities. It houses communal sitting areas, a covered terrace, offices, the pool and adjacent restaurant, and a dozen second-story accommodations.

> 🔲 **TIP**
>
> The hotel shares the bay with an inn and a few private homes so it is secluded and very private.

This is the most romantic hotel on the island.

The bulk of the accommodations are in 16 cottages and three beachfront suites. Some cottages are on the beach, but most are across the road in a garden area, where there is an additional pool. All the rooms still feature antique mahogany furniture, but the colorful fabrics have been replaced by white on the walls, the floors and the bed furnishings. The contrast is appealing. The rooms are individually furnished, but many have antique prints collected from neighboring islands. All are large and have air-conditioning, ceiling fans and stocked mini-bars. A few garden cottages have kitchenettes.

Some suites have Jacuzzis.

Isle de France has the best sports facilities on the island, including two spacious pools, tennis courts, an air-conditioned squash court (the only one on St. Barts) and a fitness center. A watersports center is on the beach and a ranch nearby offers horseback riding. You can also jog on the long, quiet beach.

A poolside gazebo houses the **La Case de L'Isle** restaurant, which serves lunch and dinner. Its French-born chef is known for light

French dishes. You can order from room service (24 hours) and dine privately on your terrace. The restaurant is open to the public. Continental breakfast is included in your rate.

Le Toiny

Anse de Toiny
St. Barts, FWI 97133
☎ 590-27-88-88; fax 590-27-89-30;
www.letoiny.com
Deluxe

Many would select Le Toiny, a member of the Relais & Chateaux, as St. Barts' most luxurious hideaway. Brad Pitt and Gwenyth Paltrow are among those that did. What is most striking about this 12-villa retreat is how determined the owners, architects and interior decorators were to insure guest privacy and comfort. The green peaked rooftops, each on a different level, sit on a secluded promontory overlooking St. Barts' rugged southern coast.

Closed Sept. 1 through Oct. 20.

The main building at the head of the driveway houses a small formal lobby decorated with dark woods and pillowed settees. The fashionable **Le Gaic restaurant** (see *Dining,* page 90) adjoins the lobby, as does a semi-circular pool and large sundeck. Non-guests who eat lunch at the restaurant may also use this pool. Hotel guests in the one- , two- and three-bedroom suites have private pools and sundecks and the most luxuriously furnished accommodations on St. Barts. They offer polished floors, four-poster beds with mosquito netting, a fax/telephone, satellite TV and VCR, stocked mini-bar, a

No swimming here, but board surfers take advantage of the rolling waves.

kitchenette with microwave and icemaker, porcelain vases filled with fresh flowers and a stationary bike. Bathrooms, too, are exceptional, with walk-in closets, hand-milled soaps and sunken tubs.

The ultimate luxury is the continental breakfast served each morning on your private terrace, with fresh tropical fruits and juices, flaky croissants and muffins, yogurt and your favorite beverages on fine china.

Grand Cul de Sac and Salines Beaches are just five minutes away, as are tennis courts. If you have to ask how much it costs, you probably can't afford it. But, if you can, it's truly exceptional.

Hotel Manapany Cottages
Box 114, Anse des Cayes
St. Barts, FWI 97133
☎ 590-27-66-55; fax 590-27-75-28;
www.lemanapany.com
Expensive-Deluxe

Open all year.

The steep road to Anse des Cayes, a secluded cove on a rugged coast, is lined by unruly palm trees and thick tropical plants. This "return-to-nature" theme is enhanced by the roar of waves that pound the rocks at the edge of the main house and gourmet restaurant. One would expect a rustic resort, so it is a surprise to find such a luxurious one. Forty-six accommodations are scattered throughout the hotel's 2½ acres. The newest and most luxurious are on the beach, while the majority (20) are in attached red-roofed cottages built on the hillside overlooking the beach and surrounded by trees and gardens.

The dozen "club suites" are decorated in marine, Asian and Caribbean themes, with large marble baths, full kitchens and living/dining areas with glass sliding doors open to the terrace. The hillside cottages are smaller but charmingly decorated as well. Families can ask for an adjoining unit to be converted into a single accommodation (it raises but does not double the cost). Hillside cottages have kitchen-ettes on their terraces.

Anse des Cayes is a lovely beach which is virtu-ally private. The hotel has placed white umbrella-capped tables and lounge chairs on the beach and around the oval pool. The watersports center has gear for snorkeling and windsurfing. There is a tennis court and fitness center.

Manapany has an excellent Italian restaurant called **Fellini**. Another good restaurant – **New Born** – is also on the cove. Hotel guests gather at the piano bar after dinner.

Carl Gustaf Hotel

Rue des Normands, Gustavia
St. Barts, FWI 97133
☎ 590-29-79-00; fax 590-27-82-37;
www.carlgustaf.com
Deluxe

The only deluxe hotel located in the capital, the Carl Gustaf is an all-suite gem notched into a hillside at the foot of the harbor. Red-tile roofs

Closed Sept.

top the pale orange buildings, which are enveloped by flowering plants and terraced walkways. There are 14 suites. All, whether one- or two-bedroom, have a private terrace and plunge pool. The living room has whitewashed walls and French doors that open onto the terrace. Décor includes rough marble floors and wicker furniture with colorful nautical and tropical prints. In-room amenities include well-appointed kitchenettes, stocked mini-bars, fax machines, satellite TV and VCR, and a stereo. There is 24-hour room service, a fitness center and a pool. The **Carl Gustaf restaurant** (see page 92) is one of the island's best. You can walk into town to shop or eat and the hotel has shuttle service to nearby beaches.

Hotel Christopher
Box 571, Pointe Milou
St. Barts, FWI 97098
☎ 590-27-63-63; fax 590-27-92-92;
www.st-barths.com/christopher-hotel
Expensive

Closed Sept. 1 through Oct. 15

Large by St. Barts standards, the 40-room Christopher spreads along secluded Milou Point on the island's northeast coast. The shoreline is rocky and there is no beach, but you can swim or cool off in the irregularly shaped pool that abuts the shore. Very large, it is encircled and divided into segments by a woodplank sundeck. Small footbridges lead from one area to the other. Comfortable lounge chairs are scattered throughout, many shaded by thatched umbrellas. If you want to enjoy some watersports you can head to Lorient or Cul-du-Sac beaches nearby.

Accommodations in slate-roofed, two-story attached buildings are set in a semi-circle on the nearby hillside, surrounded by a tropical garden. The green rooftops slope to provide shade for the second-level terraces and the ground-floor patios. All rooms face the sea. They are large and modern in décor. The carved woods on the bedposts and bureaus are crafted from local trees with coordinated floral accessories. Tiled baths have excellent lighting. All rooms are air-conditioned and have stocked mini-bars. You can join the daily aerobics class or work out solo in the fitness center.

Breakfast, which is included in your rate, is served at poolside or in your room. **L'Orchidée** is the gourmet French eaterie that draws many islanders for Norwegian salmon blinis or Caribbean sea bass. It sits at the water's edge.

Part of the Sofitel chain, the Christopher is one of St. Barts' most attractive stops.

Eden Rock
St. Jean
St. Barts, FWI 97133
☎ 590-29-79-99; fax 590-27-88-37;
www.edenrockhotel.com
Expensive

It's easy to see why Rémy de Haenen, the first man to land a plane on St. Barts and also its first mayor, built Eden Rock, St. Barts' first hotel, on this steep rocky promontory that juts

Open all year.

into St. Jean Bay like a giant exclamation point. It is dramatic to look at and it breaks the beach into two strips. Built in the 1950s, it was sorely in need of loving care by the 1990s. Fortunately, a young British couple, Jane and David Matthews, and their two young children, purchased the property in 1995. They have made many changes, some necessary and others to upgrade and expand the facilities. They have not changed the hotel's essential character.

The 10 original rooms, six on the rock and four on the beach, have all been renovated. Four new suites have been added. Each room is individually furnished, but they all have terra cotta floors, four-poster beds, print fabrics and lots of British antiques. Some have terraces. They have also reopened the hilltop bar and the **Top of the Rock restaurant**, which are first-rate. Breakfast, which is included, is served in your room.

An open-air tapas bar has become a popular watering hole. You can watch the sunset over St. Jean beach. There are two restaurants near the swimming pool.

The **Eden Rock Spa** is the most elegant on St. Barts and it offers a wide range of beauty treatments and exercise gear. The new watersports center is stocked with all manner of water toys and you don't have to be a hotel guest to rent them.

Because Eden Rock is home to the Matthews family, you'll see watercolors by Jane and her children around the hotel.

Hotel François Plantation

Colombier
St. Barts, FWI 97133
☎ 590-29-80-22; fax 590-27-61-26;
www.st-barths.com/francois-plantation
Expensive

Closed Aug. 1 through Oct. 3.

In 1987, François Beret, a well-known local chef, purchased a manor house on a hilltop on the island's north fork near the village of Colombier. He used the spacious grounds to create an intimate cottage resort that is off-beat both in location and ambience. Although the grounds are large enough to support scores of cottages, the Berets were determined to build a peaceful retreat and therefore built only a dozen, widely spaced and enveloped by lush gardens, where birds sing and where gourmet dining and imbibing are key ingredients.

▣ TIP

The gourmet restaurant is reviewed in the *Best Places to Eat* section, page 88. Even if you don't stay here, you can enjoy dinner here one night.

The main building retains its Colonial architecture and is painted in traditional blue, pink and yellow pastel tones. It has a wrap-around terrace with pillowed wicker chairs and couches where hotel guests and those dining at the restaurant congregate and sip aperitifs. The inner lobby is quite large, with dark woods and carved mahogany tables and chairs with high cane backs. There are floral settees throughout and lots of green plants as well. The François Plantation is known for its first-rate wine cellar, which is open to the public on request.

There are 10 individual cottages and two cottages that can be reconfigured to suit a family of six. You'll find fresh flowers in each cottage as well as a queen-sized bed, Caribbean art, colorful fabrics and a stocked mini-bar. Each has a private terrace (eight face the sea), which has unusual lounge chairs. Each also offers its own parking spot.

The sea is a short downhill hike away.

The plantation's pool sits at the top of the resort overlooking nearby beaches and the coast.

> ### 🔲 TIP
>
> François Plantation is in a residential area and is not within easy walking distance of any beach or town. A car is a must.

Le Tom Beach
St. Jean Beach
St. Barts, FWI 97133
☎ 590-27-53-13; fax 590-27-53-15;

Le Tom Beach is the newest luxury hotel on the island.

www.frenchcaribbean.com/TomBeach.html
Expensive-Deluxe
This nondescript building sits roadside and even the small and sparsely furnished lobby is

unimpressive. But when you exit onto the beautifully landscaped grounds, you see why this hotel is so popular. The 12 modern rooms are in two-story buildings scattered throughout the property and on the beach itself. Deluxe second-story rooms facing the sea have private terraces and lower-level rooms have patios. Rooms are air-conditioned and also have ceiling fans and mosquito netting around the king-size bed just in case you prefer open windows. Large tiled bathrooms.

Closed Sept.

Buildings are connected by boardwalk-style plank paths which also lead to the pool, restaurant and beach. Rates include continental breakfast. The restaurant serves breakfast and lunch. Non-guests eating lunch can also use the pool.

Filao Beach Hotel
Box 667, St. Jean Bay
St. Barts, FWI 97009
☎ 590-27-64-84; fax 590-27-62-24;
www.st-barths.com/filao-beach
Expensive

Closed Sept. 1 through Oct. 17.

St. Jean Beach is the hub of action on St. Barts and the Filao Beach Hotel is the center of the hub. Its seaside bar and restaurant are often crowded with beachgoers. Those eating lunch at the restaurant can also use the pool. Windsurfers, sand volleyball players and joggers keep the beach busy and noisy from early in the morning till dusk. The hotel is an easy stroll to the town, to shops and to restaurants.

A member of the prestigious Small Luxury Hotels of the World group, the hotel has 30 rooms. These are all at ground level, set in a horseshoe shape in a lovely garden. Virtually every type of tree and flower that flourishes in the Caribbean has been nurtured here, and they are all labeled. You'll skirt lily ponds en route to your cottage, marked by a colorful ceramic owl.

Deluxe suites face the beach while superior rooms are in the garden just a few steps away. Furnishings are Caribbean-style, not spectacular but well maintained. Breakfast and airport transfers are included in your rate.

You can sit on your terrace and watch the tiny planes land at the airport across the bay.

El Sereno Beach Hotel

Grand Cul de Sac
St. Barts, FWI 97133

Closed Sept. 1 through Oct. 15.

☎ 590-27-64-80; fax 590-27-75-47;
www.st-barths.com/sereno-beach
Moderate-Expensive

El Sereno is one of St. Barts' most popular hotels. Its appeal is obvious. It has a fabulous location on the bay side of Grand Cul de Sac, and its sandy beach is both long and wide. There's an offshore coral reef that even beginning snorkelers can enjoy.

It has recently refurbished 19 of its garden bungalows and has added five new beachfront junior suites to the nine previously built. Walls are painted in pastel tones and the furnishings are contemporary with red checks and florals on the beds, comfortable armchairs and curtains. Suites have terraces facing the sea while bungalows have flower-filled patios. Hammocks sway beneath the shady palm trees. All accommodations are air-conditioned, have stocked mini-bars, color TVs and VCRs and large bathrooms.

What makes El Sereno stand out is that, in spite of its being "serene," as its name suggests, it just bursts with activity day and night. It has a large freshwater pool and the sundeck and beach have lounge chairs. Nearby, the hotel's watersports center has windsurfers, Jet Skis, Hobie Cats, canoes and snorkel gear. It can arrange for scuba diving trips. You can play tennis or work on your pecs in the well-equipped fitness center. The rolling waves take the place of workout videos. Continental breakfast is included.

Boubou's, covered with a roof but open-sided, sits at poolside and offers market-fresh garden salads and fish at lunch. The dinner menu is Mediterranean and North African dishes predominate. The site of a popular music festival every August, Boubou's has live music on weekends and a great DJ nightly.

El Sereno has built a small villa community nearby (see page 82), but it also has a special villa (called Seba) on property. Seba has two bedrooms, a large living/dining area and a fully equipped kitchen. The terrace faces Marigot Bay. Guests have full hotel privileges.

Saint-Barth's Beach Hotel

Box 580, Grand Cul de Sac
St. Barts, FWI 97098
☎ 590-27-60-70; fax 590-27-75-57;
www.saintbarthbeachhotel.com
Moderate

If you need elegant furnishings and a host of amenities to enjoy your vacation, then the Saint-Barth's Beach Hotel is not the place for you. This is one of the island's older hotels, and it is comfortable rather than elegant. It does, however, offer many amenities.

The hotel has a wonderful location on Grand Cul de Sac, with a wide sandy beach on the sheltered side of the cove. It has the best watersports center on the island for windsurfers, with a school for beginning and advanced surfers. They also rent surfboards, Hobie Cats, waterskis, Jet Skis and sunning mats. Non-guests can rent equipment as well (the center does not belong to the hotel). **Le Rivage** (see *Dining*, page 101) is an excellent restaurant. There is a large pool, a sundeck, a tennis court and a fitness center.

There are eight attached villas as you enter the hotel grounds. Just a few steps from the beach and pool, they have kitchenettes, one or two air-conditioned bedrooms and ceilings fans else-where. Each has a small terrace and barbecue. Furnishings are worn but comfortable. The majority of the rooms (36) are in the main building on the beach. All are air-conditioned and have TV, VCR and a small terrace. This hotel is a very good choice for those with young children. You can easily walk or jog to El Sereno Hotel nearby.

> ### 🔲 TIP
> The hotel offers several special package deals. Inquire before making your reservation.

Saint-Barth's Beach Hotel has a separate villa community, Residence Saint Barth on Petit Cul de Sac near the luxurious Le Toiny hotel.

Village St. Jean
Box 623, St. Jean
St. Barts, FWI 97098
☎ 590-27-61-39; fax 590-27-77-96;
www.villagestjeanhotel.com
Inexpensive-Moderate/Expensive

Open year-round.

Pioneers when they built Village St. Jean 17 years ago, the Charneau family, originally from Guadeloupe, continues to oversee the resort today. Père Charneau wanted a village effect so he constructed cottages in a semi-circle across this rolling hill that overlooks St. Jean Beach and the airport. Stone paths that crisscross the grounds connect the cottages to the main house, restaurant and pool.

There are some rooms in the main building, which is marked by a small bustling lobby where Catherine Charneau holds court. She grew up here and her island tips are invaluable. These rooms are the least expensive accommodations. They have twin beds, small sitting areas and terraces with kitchenette facilities that face the beach.

The newly refurbished cottages have one or two bedrooms with king-sized beds, teak and cane furniture, floral bedspreads and blue tiled baths. Private garden patios or terraces front each lodging. Each has a fully equipped open-air kitchen area, lounge chairs and hammocks. There are 25 rooms in all.

The grounds are beautifully landscaped and the large sundeck that surrounds the pool has a waterfall and Jacuzzi. It is the meeting point for guests. **Terrazza**, the on-property restaurant, serves breakfast and has take-out service should you prefer to dine on your terrace. A great location, only a few minutes walk from the beach and La Villa Créole Shopping Center, makes this an excellent choice.

Terrazza serves Italian food. It's closed Wednesdays.

Tropical Hotel
St. Jean Bay
St. Barts, FWI 97133
☎ 590-27-64-87; fax 590-27-81-74;
www.st-barths.com/tropical-hotel
Moderate-Expensive

Closed May 31-July 15.

Small and intimate, more like a country inn than a hotel, the Tropical has a terrific location on a hillside that overlooks St. Jean Bay. It is adjacent to the Village St. Jean Hotel. A five-minute stroll (downhill) brings you to the beach, several inexpensive restaurants, and a shopping mall, La Villa Créole.

The 20 cottages, built like typical *cases*, are set around a central courtyard. Some face the bay and others the flower-filled garden. Many have private terraces. They've been redecorated with whitewashed walls, air conditioners, TV (no satellite) and white headboards that feature carved pineapples. Comfortable but not elegant. Continental breakfast (included) is served in the garden lounge and there is a small bar serving light food at the pool and sundeck. In high season, a local band plays at happy hour. Children under four stay free.

Nice spot, but overpriced compared to others.

Hotel Emeraude Plage
Baie de Saint Jean
St. Barts, FWI 97133
☎ 590-27-64-78; fax 590-27-83-08;
www.emeraudeplage.com
Moderate

Open all year.

Emeraude Plage is an informal hotel that is well-run and well-maintained, and so it has a loyal repeat following. Guests congregate in the comfortable lobby, which is furnished with bamboo couches and chairs covered in bold Native American patterned prints.

🔲 TIP

A focal point here is the used-book library filled with books on many subjects and in many languages. Guests borrow from and replenish the supply.

The hotel is on St. Jean Beach, the island's most popular sand strip, and guests use the water-sports centers and many restaurants on the beach (Emeraude Plage has no private facilities, not even a pool).

Lodging consists of 24 comfortable and spacious cottages, three suites (two-bedroom) and one deluxe villa (two-bedroom/two-bath). Scattered through the property, they are shaded by sea-grape trees, which also provide a measure of privacy from beach passersby and from one cottage to the other. Cottages are whitewashed with peaked beamed ceilings and colorful fabrics. Air-conditioned, each has an equipped kitchenette on its terrace and daily maid service. A good choice for self-starters.

Hostellerie des Trois Forces
Vitet
St. Barts, FWI 97133

Closed July.

☎ 590-27-61-25; fax 590-27-81-38;
www.3forces.net
Inexpensive

Whether you are an Aquarian or a Leo, you will enjoy this tiny (eight-room) inn owned by a St. Barts character, Hubert Delamotte. He is the island astrologer and while we don't know first-hand, lore has it that he is very fluent and very funny in French, English and German. The cottages are on a hilltop in a secluded part of the island. Each is decorated in West Indies style and according to astrological color schemes. Each has air-conditioning and a terrace with a view of the ocean. There are four-poster beds and furnishings specific to the astrological sign of that room. The restaurant offers French cuisine with many vegetarian dishes. There is a small pool. Stop in for a drink at the bar as you explore the island.

Small Hotels & Inns

La Banane
Baie de Lorient
St. Barts, FWI 97133
☎ 590-52-03-00; fax 590-27-68-44;
www.labanane.com
Moderate

Although it has a terrific location and natural ambience, La Banane was not included in the first edition of this guide. It had fallen into disrepair and the owners seemed to have few plans for it. We're happy to report that they sold it and the new owners have refurbished the main building and all nine cottages have been redecorated. Contemporary furniture, colorful fabrics and modern accessories such as TVs, DVDs and mini-bars have been added. All are air-conditioned. In an unusual quirk, the doors to the individual patios lead from the modern bathrooms. The grounds, with stately palms and lush tropical gardens, have been cut back and carefully tended so the two pools and picturesque cottages stand out. A path leads to Lorient Beach, a five-minute walk away. One of the island's loveliest sand strips, it is rarely crowded.

Baie des Anges

Box 162, Flamands
St. Barts, FWI 97133
☎ 590-27-63-61; fax 590-27-83-44;
www.st-barths.com/baie-des-anges
Moderate

Closed Sept.

The 10-room Baie des Anges is one of St. Barts' newest stops and a fine choice for families with young children. It is owned by the Ange family, with Annie Ange keeping a watchful eye on everything. Each contemporary unit is air-conditioned, but has ceiling fans as well. The bedroom has a king-size bed and there is also a sleeper sofa. All are equipped with TV sets, telephones and full kitchenettes. Since all units face Flamands Beach, children are just a few steps from a giant playground. There is also a pool. **La Langouste**, the restaurant, is at pool-side. It serves breakfast, lunch and dinner, with a French-Creole tilt at dinner. It is best known for its lobsters, which draw diners from the deluxe St. Barth Isle de France Hotel, also on Flamands Beach. Ask Annie to arrange for you to use their tennis court and fitness center (for a fee).

La Résidence Les Lataniers

Anse des Cayes
St. Barts, FWI 97133
☎ 590-27-80-84; fax 590-27-78-45
Moderate

Open all year.

Les Lataniers is not an exciting stop when compared to other hotels on the island, but it is an excellent choice for families not needing resort amenities. Hidden from view by flowering vines and luxuriant greenery, the gingerbread-trimmed cottages with turquoise roofs and terra cotta walls are on a hill high above lovely Anse des Cayes Beach. Although management has changed, it is still family-owned and the property is beautifully maintained. Each of the sparkling 12 units is a suite with a king- or queen-sized bed and a sofa that can sleep two children. The blue and coral tropical rattan and wicker furniture is user friendly and each air-conditioned room has a TV, VCR and tiled bathroom. There is a fully equipped kitchenette so you can prepare your own meals (although you can also order breakfast from the hotel). You will enjoy the view from your private terrace and you can swim in the good-sized pool. There is a seven-night minimum stay requirement.

回 TIP

Because of its out-of-the-way location, a car is a must here.

Manoir de Saint Barthelemy
Lorient
St. Barts, FWI 97133
☎ 590-27-79-27; fax 590-27-65-75
Inexpensive

Open all year.

Looking for something a little different? How about a bed and breakfast St. Barts style? A 17th-century Norman country house is the hub of this colony started by French artists. Rather than a room in someone's home and a bathroom down the hall, you'll have your own cottage (with one to three bedrooms), king-sized beds, kitchenette, ceiling fans and full baths. The grounds are lovely, filled with mango and papaya trees, hammocks and a small waterfall that replenishes a pond stocked with tropical fish and plants. You can easily walk to the beach. There is a mini-mart in town but no restaurant nearby. Breakfast is served in your room or in the main house.

Les Mouettes

Lorient Beach
St. Barts, FWI 97133
☎ 590-27-77-91; fax 590-27-68-19;
www.cieux.com/lesm.html
Inexpensive

Open all year.

There is a mini-mart across the road should you want to cook. The seven air-conditioned rooms are furnished in motel style with two beds, a dresser and table that is both a desk and dining area. The bathroom is sans tub. A plus is the kitchenette with stove, refrigerator and utensils. A small terrace faces the beach. There is daily maid service. This is as basic as it gets on St. Barts – despite its location on Lorient Beach, the best surfing beach on the island.

MC/Visa accepted, but only reluctantly.

Les Islets Fleuris

Open all year.

Hauts de Lorient
St. Barts, FWI 97133
☎ 590-27-64-22; fax 590-27-69-72;
www.st-barths.com/islets-fleuris
Inexpensive

Another simple choice for people who don't intend to spend much time indoors, Les Islets

Fleuris is in the hills above Lorient. Your accommodation will be a small cottage with a comfortable bed enclosed by mosquito netting, a bathroom with a shower only, a fully equipped kitchenette and a comfortable terrace facing the garden or the sea. One of the cottages offers a living room, and there are a total of six studios and one suite. There is a small pool on the property. A small charge is made for breakfast and for a TV/VCR.

Villa Rentals

There are a number of reasons villa rentals are a very popular alternative on St. Barts. Many celebrity visitors opt for the privacy and serenity offered by villas, while families with children enjoy the home-away-from-home feeling, with extra space, and without the headaches. A very practical reason why villas are so popular is because there are only 600 or so rooms available on St. Barts at any one time, and it can be difficult to get space during holidays and in the high season. And finally, but certainly not insignificantly, is the idea that you can save quite a bit of money, especially if you have a large family or can share a spacious villa with friends or family members.

Keep in mind that villas run the gamut from a one-bedroom on the beach to a five-bedroom pad with a private pool and everything in between. Rental agencies will send you a complete listing of what is available.

Hotel Villa Communities

Two hotels have built "villa" communities near their properties. These are very different from private villas. They are hotel-type accommodations without major amenities, but they do offer full use of hotel facilities.

Les Résidences Saint Barth are five minutes from the hotel by car. There are 20 villas (one- to three-bedroom), seven of which have private pools. All have private terraces, fully equipped kitchens and modern baths. They are in attached two-story buildings with ocean views. Contact them at Petit Cul de Sac, St. Barts, FWI 97098. ☎ 27-85-93; fax 27-77-59. www.st-barths.com/stbarths-beach-hotel/ sbbh_residences.html.

Owned by St. Barth Beach Hotel.

El Sereno Villas are just off the main road at the turn-off to Grand Cul de Sac and two minutes from the hotel by car. There are nine one-bedroom villas in air-conditioned units with full kitchens. Contact El Sereno Hotel, Grand Cul de Sac, St. Barts, FWI 97133. ☎ 27-64-80; fax 27-75-47.

Villa rental rates vary according to the available facilities, the season, and the number of bedrooms you need. Generally speaking, you should figure two people to a bedroom. For villa rentals, the high season runs from December 15 through April 15. There is normally a one-week minimum stay required, and a 10-day minimum between Christmas and New Year's. Off-season rates are reduced by up to 40%.

Rental Agencies

The largest agency is **Sibarth Villas** on rue du Centenaire in Gustavia. ☎ 29-88-90; fax 27- 60-52. They are represented by WIMCO (West Indies Management Co.). In the US, ☎ 800-932-3222 or fax 401-847-6290. www2.wimco.com/stbarthelemy.asp.

Another well respected agency, **St. Barth Properties**, has over 100 villas to rent and for sale. They are on rue du Centenaire, near the Post Office. ☎ 590-29-75-05. In the US, 800-421-3396. www.stbarth.com.

St. Barth Dream Vacations, rue du Centenaire, Gustavia, is still another option. ☎ 29-75-05; fax 29-72-03. www.st-barths.com/stbarth-dream.

Sprimbarth Real Estate is the agency for the stunning villas in Les Jardins de St. Jean, a community on the hillside above town. ☎ 27-67-70; fax 27-84-40.

MountainWaves has luxury villas on St. Barts and St. Martin. ☎ 888-349-7800, www.mountainwaves.com.

Also try **Ici Et La** on Quai de la Républic, Gustavia. ☎ 27-78-78 or fax 27-78-28.

Best Places to Eat

St. Barts, a very small island, is home to over 50 independent restaurants, one for every one hundred residents. Several would stand out in Paris or New York. These are either owned by European-trained local chefs, or make use of hired master chefs from France to oversee their kitchens. A few of the exceptional restaurants are in hotels. There are bistros, brasseries, rotisseries and cafés as well. Visiting gourmets can be adventurous both in cuisine and ambience.

Most menus feature French cuisine using oysters flown in from Brittany, pâtés and cheeses from Provence and wines from other parts of France. Meats and fresh produce are imported from the US, while fish and shellfish are often from local waters. Preparation varies from traditional to nouvelle and there are some Creole dishes, too. Those featuring the local spiny lobster (langouste) lead the list. Continental restaurants have eclectic menus that roam the globe, blending tapas from Spain with pastas from Italy and lots of Southeast Asian specialties.

▣ TIP

Because so many items are imported, you'll find the restaurants pricey, but even the most expensive eateries will have a good value prix-fixe menu. By selecting carefully, you can keep your costs down.

Restaurants are informal and relaxed. Their ambience comes from a stunning location at seaside or atop a hill that overlooks the coast. You can dine on a tree-filled patio, in a flowered garden or on a quaint capital street. Music, whether live or on CD, is more often Mozart than Marley. Good food, fine wines and lovely settings all combine to slow your inner clock.

Dining Hours

Restaurants, even those in hotels, serve lunch from noon until 3 pm, then close until 6 or 7 pm, when most re-open to serve dinner until 10 or 11 pm. An interesting dining phenomenon here are the gourmet beachside restaurants that serve lunch only. We will detail them for you. Most gourmet restaurants serve only dinner (we will detail many of those as well). European visitors and locals enjoy long leisurely lunches, making it the day's main meal. North American visitors crowd the better restaurants at night. Never fear! You won't go hungry. There are cafés and small restaurants that stay open from early morning till late at night.

Dining Savvy

- ◉ Restaurants are small. Reservations are a must in-season and a good idea year-round.
- ◉ Restaurants add a 15% service charge to your bill so you should not tip an additional 15%. It is common

to leave a small additional tip if the service was good.

◎ Many of the better restaurants close for a time in the off-season. Closings vary. If your first choice is closed, you'll still have many options.

◎ Most restaurants accept major credit cards, but a few small local spots do not. These are noted in the text. You can also pay in US dollars, but you will get change in euros.

◎ Casual chic attire is the norm at lunch and dinner. Shorts and bathing suits are okay at beachside or poolside spots. Jackets are rare; ties are unheard of.

◎ Almost every menu has a vegetarian dish or two.

Alive Price Scale

Designed to give you some idea of prices, the Alive Scale is based on a three-course dinner for one person without drinks, service or sales tax.

Very Expensive . . . . over $70

Expensive . . . . $50-$70

Moderate . . . . $35-$49

Inexpensive . . . . under $35

Lunch prices are lower.

Exceptional Dining Spots

L'Esprit Salines

Salines

☎ 52-46-10

Visa, Mastercard only

Expensive

We have friends who have spent the week between Christmas and New Years on St. Barts for the last 15 years. Clearly they love the island and they particularly love the food. Many of the offbeat restaurants in the first edition of this guide (not found in other books) were suggested by them. When they raved about L'Esprit, we knew it must be special and it was.

While many of St. Barts' finest restaurants are set in hotels (although independently owned), L'Esprit Salines sits adjacent to the Salines salt flats and beach. A dozen wooden tables and a small bar are set on a wooden platform covered by a circular dome. The "walls" are open to allow for the cooling breezes, but plastic shades can be lowered should it rain. Multi-colored flowers and aromatic trees encircle the platform.

Lunch and dinner are served daily (except Tuesday). The lunch menu changes seasonally. It has a variety of salads, soups and fish, chicken and lamb dishes – much more a European-style lunch than an American one.

L' Esprit draws both locals and visitors – most are French-speaking. The staff is fluent in English.

It is the dinner menu (printed in French and English) that garners attention. It is small, changes nightly, is and leans toward French-Asian specialties. The Vietnamese-style prawns ravioli, served with a variety of dipping sauces, is the restaurant's signature dish. It is often on the menu and is delicious. A soup (zucchini or carrot), a salad, a crab cassolette and a variety of cheeses are other openers. Provençal-style grilled scallops, sautéed chicken and veal with black mushrooms or a Vietnamese-style mahi-mahi are among the regular choices. Vegetables served separately include mashed carrots with curry and Cyprus-style potatoes.

Closed Tuesday.

There is a vegetarian plate nightly as well. Desserts are heavy on fruit tarts and chocolate cakes, but take heart – portions aren't huge.

Salines is well off the beaten track and L'Esprit's closest neighbors are the unique birds resting on the salt flats. They provide the background music to a lovely evening. Reservations are a must year-round.

Route des Espices
François Plantation, Colombier
☎ 27-78-82
Very Expensive
Dinner Only

Typically, where we find an exceptional hotel there is a fine restaurant on the premises. Here we find an exceptional restaurant that has a hotel built around it. Owner François Beret made his name on St. Barts as the chef at several gourmet restaurants. In 1984 the Berets decided to open a place of their own and selected a Colonial manor house near Colombier. They built 12 typical St. Barts cottages for guests, planted wonderful gardens and renovated the manor house to serve as the hotel lobby, a breakfast nook and a cocktail/tea lounge. The wrap-around terrace has comfortable wicker chairs and couches where diners wait for tables or enjoy after-dinner drinks.

Closed Aug. 1 through Oct. 15 and Sundays.

The restaurant, reached via a flower-filled arborway, looks like a formal living room with carved mahogany tables, high-backed chairs and white latticed place mats. Mr. Beret is no longer the primary chef, but he continues to work with the French chefs he hires to prepare dishes in his preferred nouvelle style.

Start with goat cheese ravioli, mussel soup or foie gras, then continue with breast of duck with mangoes and ginger, sweet and sour rack of lamb or scallops sautéed and rolled in pan-fried rice.

★ DID YOU KNOW?

A specialty of the restaurant is *coutancie*, beef from cattle that are fed beer every day and have their bodies rubbed down twice daily. It's incredibly tender.

One of the best desserts is a chocolate tart with vanilla ice cream. François Plantation is arguably St. Barts' finest restaurant.

Le Gaic

Toiny (Toiny Hotel)

☎ 27-88-88

Very Expensive

Lunch & dinner, Buffet lunch on Sunday.

Closed Tuesday off-season and from Sept. 1 through Oct. 20.

It's difficult to imagine a formal dining room that is adjacent to a swimming pool and sundeck and where the background "music" is the sound of waves crashing into the shore. But Le Gaic is just that and it would be right at home if it were suddenly transported to New York or Paris. The tables are covered with rich blue fabric, the fine china is white with matching blue trim and the stemware is blue as well. High-back navy blue chairs are placed at each table. The menu is classic French, but a few Creole touches and ingredients creep in.

Le Gaic's terrace is partly open-air and partly roof-covered and fan-cooled. At lunch, many guests select the informal open-air tables and take a swim after lunch. There is a prix-fixe lunch and such à la carte items as chilled mango soup, shrimp salad with spicy yogurt dressing, scrambled eggs or smoked sliced chicken with gingered grilled vegetables.

Dinner is a lot more formal, both in ambience (dim lights, music) and menu. Smoked salmon with vegetable blinis, conch ravioli with garlic sauce or duck carpaccio are great openers. Main courses include rack of lamb in a clay shell with sweet potatoes, hen stuffed with wild mushrooms, and shrimp wrapped and fried with a peppered red wine sauce.

You can linger after dinner and enjoy aperitifs on the sundeck, now moon-lit and star-covered. Le Gaïc vies with François Plantation as St. Barts' finest. It's a special spot for a special occasion.

Chez Maya
Public Beach
☎ 27-75-73
Moderate-Expensive
Dinner only; closed Sundays

Maya's makes the point that it's the food that counts. If the food is good enough, people will come. And they do – in bunches – both locals and celebrities and ordinary visitors like us who've read about this innovative restaurant in a spate of articles in both travel and food magazines.

Closed June & Sept.

Randy and Maya Gurley opened their roof-covered, open-terrace eaterie on Public Beach near Gustavia, not the best location on St. Barts. They installed white formica tables and multi-colored director's chairs and lots of flowers. Then they let the innovative, delicious dishes speak for themselves. Maya, the chef, was born on Martinique, where she mastered French cooking. The heart of the menu is French, as are the wines. But over the years Maya has expanded her horizons to include Creole, as well as Thai, Vietnamese and other Oriental dishes. The menu, which changes nightly, is always a blend of cuisines. Each night Maya and her staff prepare five appetizers, five entrées and five desserts.

🔲 TIP

Decisions are hard to make, but if you have a group you can order all selections and sample a bit of each.

Favorites include tomato and mango salad, salmon teriyaki, duck à l'orange, squash fritters and curried sweet potato salad. Thick chocolate cake is a good dessert choice.

Carl Gustaf Restaurant
Rue des Normands (Carl Gustaf Hotel)
☎ 27-82-83
Very Expensive

Closed Sept. and for lunch during off-season.

Carl Gustaf is a small luxury resort notched into a hillside with a panoramic view of the capital and its harbor.

★ DID YOU KNOW?

Because of the limited space available, architects placed the tiny lobby, gourmet restaurant, pool and piano bar together on a large terrace at the hotel's highest level. It is unusual, but it works.

Guests eat lunch on the open-air terrace or the adjacent tables that are roof-covered and fan-cooled. The view is constantly changing as yachts, sailboats and ferries glide into berths at the dock. The informal menu includes lobster salad, shrimp dishes, creamed soups and grilled meats. Many diners take a dip in the pool.

By nightfall, the staff has set the tables with starched tablecloths, napkins, fine china and stemware. The view is the fabulous sunset and then a star-filled sky. The pianist arrives, the bar is crowded and the staff is immaculately attired.

The French menu has a few Creole touches. You can select your wine from their ample wine cellar. Good starters include the circle of prawns and avocados, Andalucian gazpacho or lobster spring rolls. Follow with prawn risotto, roasted salmon with vanilla sauce and sweet potato, fricassée of shellfish with pasta, lamb with crêpes and veal cutlets Provençal. Fruit tarts and crème brûlée are good desserts. This is one of the finest restaurants on St. Barts.

Gustavia

Le Sapotillier
Rue du Centenaire
☎ 27-60-28
Expensive
Dinner only

Whether you reserve an indoor table or one in the garden under a namesake sapodilla tree, you'll enjoy the experience. Look for the typical St. Barts *case* (Creole for cottage) on the street that connects the two legs of Gustavia Harbor. It looks like a private home and the service is so unrushed that it is easy to forget you are in a restaurant. Brick walls, starched white linen

Closed Sundays off-season, as well as during early May and late Oct.

cloths, gaily painted wooden chairs and color-filled Creole paintings add to your pleasure. Those seated in the garden will enjoy the cooling trade winds and starry skies.

While the décor is quite simple, the menu is anything but. Serving traditional Provençal food, Le Sapotillier is best known for its seafood dishes, particularly those using sea bass and huge shrimp. Frogs' legs fricassee or lasagne d'escargots may not sound like something Grandma made, but are actually delicious, as is the roasted Irish salmon. Those who prefer meat will enjoy the filet of beef with morels or the classic duck with peaches. There are prix-fixe French and Creole menus nightly.

🔲 TIP

Save room for the soft apple cake with ice cream. If it tastes surprisingly like strudel, it's because the owner and the chef are Austrian.

La Mandala
Rue Thiers
☎ 27-96-96
Expensive
Lunch and dinner; Sunday brunch
Location! Location! Location! La Mandala has the best location in Gustavia – on a hill overlooking the town and harbor. Opened in late 1995, just missing Hurricane Luis, the Mandala is a Buddhist symbol of harmony. The square within a circle symbol is mirrored in the restau-

rant by the square table for 10 placed above a glassed circular pool. It's striking!

The sloped beamed ceiling covers the dining terrace, which has tile floors, pillowed barrel chairs and widely spaced tables in a variety of shapes. The room's open feeling is enhanced by the music of the wind chimes.

The crowd arrives at 5 pm, vying for one of the open-air tables or a place at the bar where they enjoy the fabulous tapas and the sunset. The menu is eclectic and changes daily, mixing French, Creole and Asian dishes. Typically, you'll find salmon carpaccio, tuna sashimi, spicy Thai rolls, grilled lobster, filet of beef and even chicken soup. There is a prix-fixe menu. Lunch features salads and pastas.

La Mandala is near the Carl Gustaf Hotel and other restaurants.

Au Port
Rue du Centenaire
☎ 27-62-36
Expensive

One of the oldest restaurants on the island and among its most formal, Au Port continues to please. In a private house on the rue du Centenaire, the restaurant is on a roof-covered open porch on the second floor. Subdued indirect lighting bathes the carved mahogany chairs and pink-covered tables in a romantic hue. There are fresh flowers and green plants everywhere.

Owner/Chef Alain Bunel is a master of French/ Creole dishes and there is a Creole prix-fixe menu nightly. Conch and lobster sausages, crab and conch ravioli and the lobster casserole are staples. This is a perfect spot to sample stewed goat with curry sauce and bananas. Less adventurous? Stick to the chicken stuffed with foie gras and morel mushrooms or the filet of sole with champagne sauce. Save room for the chocolate mousse cake. Exceptional wine list.

The Wall House

Quai du Wall House, La Pointe
☎ 27-71-83; www.wall-house-stbarth.com
Moderate

A neighbor of the museum and library of the same name, the Wall House could easily be called the "White House," as it is glistening white from its wicker furniture to its tile floors, its walls and the cloths that cover tables on a roofed terrace facing the harbor. Some tables are on an outer terrace. Color is provided by tall green plants and fresh flowers strategically placed to create dining areas. The menu is French and Creole. Start with gravlax with dill sauce, gazpacho or eggplant mousse. Grilled prawns marinated in whiskey, shark in lobster sauce or beef with pepper sauce are very popular. There are two prix-fixe menus each night as well as a special lobster menu. Lunch finds grilled fish and meats, toasted sandwiches and assorted salads. This is a good choice for both lunch and dinner.

Le Resto
Rue Courbet
☎ 27-70-47
Dinner only
Moderate-Expensive

St. Barts' Italian contingent has found a niche in Gustavia's. Two excellent Italian choices are just a few blocks apart near the harbor.

Le Resto is the more formal of the two (L'Esacle, below, is the other). It is very modern in décor, with circular tables, light woods and checkered cloths. The bar takes up an entire wall and is often two-deep with patrons. The menu changes daily to take advantage of the freshest ingredients available. The pasta is made in-house and served with various sauces. There is always a risotto and the beef dishes are delicious. Save room for the chocolate cake. The sauces and seasoning here are inspired by those of Northern Italy and Provence and therefore not spicy. Dinner is served from 7 pm to midnight.

Closed Monday.

L'Escale
Rue Jeanne d'Arc, La Pointe
☎ 27-81-06
Inexpensive-Moderate
Lunch & dinner

L'Escale is more like a pizzeria. It draws people to its bar before and after dinner. On a terrace facing the harbor, it has wicker chairs, glass-topped tables and placemats. Many young locals come here after finishing work to relax at the bar and enjoy the pizzas baked in a wood-

Open daily from 11 am to midnight. Moderate.

burning oven. The specialty of the house, surprisingly, is an exceptional steak tartare. Also on the menu are lasagne, ravioli, pastas and veal dishes. The staff has worked here for many years and they are well-liked by St. Barthians.

Chez Domi

Rue Charles de Gaulle
☎ 29-84-11
Moderate
Lunch & dinner

Open all year.

Chez Domi would look right at home in St. Thomas or Tortola. It is a typical Caribbean Creole restaurant with one air-conditioned dining room and one roof-covered terrace cooled by ceiling fans. Both have deep blue tablecloths and light wood tables and chairs. Since Creole cooking relies heavily on the freshest catches and produce available, you never know what will be on the menu. If they are on offer, try stuffed crabs or garlicky baked snails for openers and West Indies fish stew in Creole sauce or crayfish with rum sauce for an entrée. Pastas are homemade. The food is delicious and the service is unhurried. A local handicraft shop is part of the restaurant.

▣ NOTE

Chez Domi now has a "snack shop" that specializes in pizza, with burgers and sandwiches as well. Take-out is available. You can call ahead. ☎ 29-85-10.

Le Vietnam
Rue du Roi Oscar II
☎ 27-81-37
Moderate-Inexpensive

Right in the heart of Gustavia, Le Vietnam, which serves both lunch and dinner, is true to its name and the nationality of its owners. It serves Vietnamese food but its extensive menu also offers Thai and Chinese dishes. The air-conditioned dining room is very attractive, with white starched tablecloths covered by thick glass, hanging Chinese lanterns, decorative red fans and large fish tanks. These fish are for decoration only, but there are many fish dishes on the menu. You'll enjoy the mahi mahi with hot and sour sauce and the crispy shrimp fritters. The soup Hanoienne with shrimp or pork is enough for an entire lunch, but hearty eaters can follow it with Vietnamese egg rolls, duck with pineapple or sweet and sour pork. You can also eat on the open terrace. Take-out is available.

Open all year.

L'Iguane
Carre d'Or Shopping Arcade
Quai de la République
☎ 27-88-46
Moderate
Open 9 am-11 pm; closed Sunday

During daylight hours L'Iguane is a café in the shopping arcade. Its umbrella-covered tables stand in the walkway. You can stop for croissants and café au lait, for ice cream, sandwiches and salads. When the sun goes down the chef

Sushi served from Nov. through May only.

rips open his shirt to reveal an "S"– no, not for superman, but for sushi and sashimi. Sushi platters include conch, shrimp, tuna and eel. Also delicious is the beef or tuna tataki (like carpaccio) and the vegetable rolls.

La Marine
Rue Jeanne d'Arc, La Pointe
☎ 27-70-13
Lunch & dinner; closed Sunday
Moderate

Closed Sept. 1-Oct. 15.

You know it's Thursday when you see scores of sailboats tied to the dock and lots of minimokes in the parking lot near La Marine. Insiders know that French shellfish arrive in St. Barts every Thursday. Oysters and mussels are the most sought after, but sardines, tuna, sole, red mullet and lobsters are also popular. Very informal.

Lorient

KFE Massai
Marche de L'Oasis
☎ 29-76-78
Dinner Only
Moderate

Closed Tuesday.

Its logo is of a dancing Masai warrior and the solid wall that encloses the restaurant seems designed to keep the lions and elephants out. We were expecting a restaurant that serves African cuisine. It doesn't, but the African influences can be found in the Creole dishes that share the menu with the more traditional French ones. Ethnic touches, in the décor and the gift shop, set the ambience.

The restaurant is set in a pebbled and palm-studded courtyard and the large bar and cocktail area just beyond the entrance is an enjoyable spot to wait for your table. A recent menu offered a tomato and mozzarella salad, a fricassée St. Jacques, scallops and shrimp in papaya sauce and an excellent filet of beef with béarnaise sauce.

Many locals come to the restaurant for desserts and coffee or after-dinner drinks. The desserts are all made in-house and include coconut sponge cake, guava fruit tart and cold sorbets.

The gift shop has a lovely selection of gifts from Africa and France.

Grand Cul de Sac

Le Rivage
St. Barths Beach Hotel
Grand Cul de Sac
☎ 28-82-42
Moderate
Lunch & dinner
Le Rivage is as close to being a "comfortable neighborhood restaurant" as it gets on St. Barts. It is built on a wooden plank boardwalk which is covered by a roof and enclosed by thick, plastic, see-through curtains that are open at

Non-guests eating lunch at Le Rivage can use the hotel's pool.

lunch and even at dinner when the temperature and the waves are right. The restaurant is just above the sandy beach and adjacent to the pool at the St. Barth Beach Hotel on Grand Cul de Sac Beach, one of the nicest on the island.

Not owned by the hotel, Le Rivage always has a respected local chef in its kitchen. Although nominally a French and Creole restaurant, the menu tilts south at dinner when you can start with sliced small salmon, shrimp with hot goat cheese or a tomato and mozzarella salad. Shrimp Créole, conch stew and chicken stew with curry sauce (which we ate several times) are all delicious. Lunch finds pastas, blood sausage and chunky lobster and crab salad. The staff is young and friendly. Good food and a relaxed dress code. You can smoke a cigar on the beach for dessert.

Boubou's
Sereno Hotel, Grand Cul de Sac
☎ 29-83-01
Moderate
Boubou, a dynamic French entrepreneur, has taken a pleasant beachside eaterie and made it a "destination." On the site of the former West Indies Café, Boubou has opened a Mediterranean restaurant with a strong North African tilt. Set on a circular, roof-covered platform, the sides are open to allow the cooling breeze in from the ocean just a few steps away. Boubou's lunch menu is heavy on salads and light platters but it is at dinner that it sparkles. Try the stuffed calamari with cumin or the iced cucum-

ber soup with yogurt. Lamb with spices, veal in a lemon sauce, chicken tajine with prunes and honey and ravioli with niçoise pesto sauce are consistent hits. Desserts are sweet, using honey and fruits. Lots of restaurants here have good food, but what lures locals and visitors alike to Boubou's is the island's best DJs. The beat is reggae, jazz or blues. You'll hear them all. Boubou and his "brother" Yannick Noah (the tennis great) started Boubou's St. Barts Festival, which is an annual event-taking place in August. Seventy musicians and DJs from all over the world take part in the 12-day event. The action is at Boubou's, but other restaurants are involved as well. Good food, lively atmosphere – year-round.

Marigot Bay Club
Marigot
☎ 27-75-45
Lunch & dinner; closed Monday
Moderate-Expensive

Marigot Bay Club is an informal restaurant just a few steps from Marigot Bay. The seafood here is as good as anywhere on the island. That's because Jean-Michel Ledee, the owner, was a working fisherman and his wife has continued to run the boat. The day's catch is the day's menu, with a few veal or chicken dishes also available.

Open all year.

The lunch crowd – often wearing bathing suits with cover-ups – arrive here before or after a morning at Marigot Beach or one of the other beaches nearby. Dinner finds many diners from nearby hotels in Bermuda-style shorts or jeans. The restaurant is very informal with a long bar area and small roof-covered terrace facing the bay. Polished wood tables and director-style chairs adorn the terrace. Lobsters, grilled or baked in the shell with gruyère cheese, are most popular. Tuna and red snapper glazed with Creole sauce are flakey and delicious. Hot goat cheese on salad greens or an appetizer portion of lobster stew are great starters.

Grande Saline

Le Colonial
Route de Saline
☎ 27-53-00
Dinner only; Amex only
Expensive

Closed Sept. 1 through Oct. 15.

One of the most attractive restaurants on St. Barts, Le Colonial is not well known because it is off the beaten track on the road from Saint Jean to Grande Saline. Set in a garden, the restaurant has a wide open feeling because it is on a covered terrace with a very high peaked roof. Its dim lighting and subdued wall hangings give it a romantic feel. The bar and cocktail areas have highly polished tables and multi-colored couches. The dining room has black lacquered tables and chairs. The décor is very dramatic.

> **◉ TIP**
>
> The chef at Le Colonial is Cambodian and the dishes are Thai, Vietnamese, Laotian and Cambodian. Look for interesting spices and lots of fish.

The Thai beef salad was enough for an entire meal, while the gingered fish rolled in a banana and seafood marmite was light and left enough room for dessert. The food is attractively served.

La Gommier
Grande Saline
☎ 87-70-57
Lunch & Dinner
Moderate

Located adjacent to the salt flats, this Creole restaurant is set in a tropical garden. Set back from the road in a traditional St. Barts "case," the ambience is enhanced by subdued lighting, starched white tablecloths, director's chairs and tanks filled with colorful fish. The menu changes daily, taking advantage of the freshest ingredients and emphasizing local seafood and lobster. La Gommier has beautiful island paintings and craftwork, as well as music. A favorite with St. Barthians.

Closed Mon-day.

```
┌─────────────────────┐
│ ▣ TIP               │
└─────────────────────┘
```

Le Grain de Sel, an informal eatery, adjoins the Salines Beach parking lot. It has indoor tables, but the best place to eat is on the open-air terrace. It serves French-Creole food and lunch is the most popular meal. Moderate. ☎ 52-46-05. Open 11:30-3 pm, 6:30-10 pm.

Le Tamarin

Grande Saline
☎ 27-72-12
Lunch & dinner; closed Monday
Dinner only to 9:30
Moderate

June through Oct., 12-4 pm only.

Grande Saline is arguably the island's loveliest beach and is certainly among the least used. It has no facilities, so locals often stop for lunch at nearby Le Tamarin. It's a funky but upscale beach eaterie with tables on a porch, in the garden or on the grass. Picnic-style tables on a sand patch are shaded by thatch umbrellas. You can sip a cool drink under the century-old tamarind tree that gives the restaurant its name or on a lounge chair or hammock, which are placed nearby. You can exchange quips with Cookie, the resident parrot who can hold his own in French and English.

Grande Saline is unofficially a nudist beach.

If you are expecting hot dogs and hamburgers – forget about it! The menu runs along the lines of carpaccios of beef and fish, chicken breast with honey and prunes, ceviche with lime and coconut or steak tartare. Apple pie and chocolate cake are good finishers. After a meal like this you have to sunbathe until you digest.

Anse Des Cayes

New Born
Anse des Cayes
☎ 27-67-07
Dinner only
Moderate
Owners Franky and David are lobster fishermen and they take great pride in the lobster dishes at their small restaurant near the Manapany Cottages Hotel. This is a terrific place to sample Creole dishes such as curried goat or shrimp and salt cod salad. A small restaurant, it has a tile floor, mauve tablecloths and wall hangings from Mexico. A large aquarium takes center stage. This informal place attracts diners from the hotel or locals.

Closed Sundays off-season.

Lunch at the Beach, St. Barts Style

Lunch is commonly the day's main meal for European visitors and for St. Barthians. That means that a burger or hot dog, fare served on most US beaches, does not cut it here. Lunch on

St. Barts brings grilled meats and fish, lobster salad, pasta and good wine. To meet the demand, an unusual dining phenomenon exists on the island. Several top-notch restaurants with beachfront locations open to serve lunch, and only lunch. They do not re-open for dinner, even though some are in hotels. Many folks spend the morning on the beach, windsurfing or playing beach volleyball, working up an appetite and a sweat. Then they head to a nearby restaurant with an adjacent pool. They take a refreshing swim, put on a T-shirt or cover-up, and sit down to a long leisurely lunch. Then they head back to the beach or home for a nap. If you want to give this a try, here are the best places to do so.

Saint Jean Beach

Filao Beach Hotel Restaurant. Lunch is served from noon until 2:30 pm. A member of the Relais & Chateaux organization, the restaurant has marble tables with a flowering cactus plant on each one. The lunch menu features chilled avocado soup, smoked local fish, lobster salad with asparagus, a marinated spicy chicken sandwich with beets, omelettes and salads. ☎ 27-64-84.

Le Plage at Tom Beach Hotel. Lunch is served from noon until 2:30 pm. The menu here is similar to that of Filao Beach Hotel, but includes grilled meats and fish, stuffed crab and hot and cold soups. ☎ 27-53-13.

Grand Cul De Sac Beach

Lafayette Club serves lunch from noon until 3:30 pm. This is a local institution where business deals are clinched here and celebrity guests are entertained. People eat here in business attire; there is a chic fashion boutique at the club as well. Barbecued lobster is king of the menu and, at $70, it should be. Duck, grilled fish and meats, goat cheese salad, pastas and more are menu staples. The piña coladas are legendary and potent, which you may appreciate when you see the check. Prices here are incredibly high. ☎ 27-62-51.

Being renovated as we go to press. Should be even more attractive when you get there.

Le Gloriette. Serves lunch from noon until 3 pm. Not as chic as its neighbor but not nearly as pricey either, Le Gloriette serves Creole dishes such as stuffed crab, goat or chicken curry, codfish critters and lobster. No credit cards. ☎ 27-75-66.

All-Day Restaurants

As previously noted, most restaurants on St. Barts serve lunch at specific hours, then close until dinner time. What's a nosher to do? Head to one of the restaurants below. They serve

from early in the morning until the wee hours –
which on St. Barts is usually 11 pm.

Gustavia

Le Repaire

No credit cards.

Rue de la République (at the port)
☎ 27-72-48
Moderate
A bustling brasserie on the harbor, Le Repaire
opens at 6 am, when crewpersons stop by for
croissants and coffee while getting their boats
ready for the day. They also serve American
breakfasts. By midday, salads and sandwiches
replace the croissants and by evening steak
frites and Creole dishes take center stage. Le
Repaire gets a shipment of French mussels and
oysters every Thursday. They rarely make it to
the weekend. An attractive stop with whitewashed walls, waffle-top tables and director's
chairs, it often has reggae music on tape. Pool
tables and live music on weekends keep La
Repaire busy till its 1 am closing (the kitchen
closes earlier).

La Crêperie

MC / Visa only.

Rue Oscar II
Hours 7 am-11 pm; closed Sunday
Inexpensive
With only a half-dozen tables inside and even
fewer on the sidewalk, you may find yourself
waiting for a table at La Crêperie. It is one of
the few restaurants that serves all day from

7 am till 11 pm. At lunch you can dig into a burger or sandwich, but everyone around you will be eating a buckwheat crêpe filled with Swiss cheese, spinach and bacon or tarragon chicken, among other fillers. If you prefer to nosh or need a late afternoon pick-me-up, you can try the wheat crêpes filled with ice cream or you can have an ice cream sundae.

Saint Jean

La Créole Restaurant and Bar
La Villa Créole Shopping Center
Hours: 7 am to 11 pm, daily
Inexpensive

Major credit cards accepted.

In the hub of the island's largest shopping center, this restaurant has indoor tables as well as tables on a terrace. They serve American-style food, including hot dogs, burgers, ham and cheese sandwiches, mushroom and cheese omelettes and roast chicken.

KiKi-e Mo
Le Plage Pelican, St. Jean
Hours: 9:30 am-7: 30 pm
A small, clean restaurant with an open-air dining terrace that serves Italian specialties. Vegetable and pasta salads, pastas and sandwiches are freshly prepared. Take-out as well.

Route de Saline

The Coffee Shop
Route de Saline
Hours: 8 am-6 pm

*Closed
Sunday.*

St. Barts' premier coffee-roaster. You can order Brazilian, Ethiopian or Costa Rican coffee, among others, with your breakfast or lunch. Wrap sandwiches are the house specialty.

Picnic Fare

Want to spend the day on the beach? Pick up picnic food at the **La Rotisserie** shop nearest to your hotel. They sell roast chicken, French and local sausage, pâtés, tabbouleh, salads, sandwiches, cheeses, quiches, freshly baked bread and pastries. Pizza, too. The main store is in Gustavia on rue du Roi Oscar II (☎ 27-63-13). A branch is in the Centre Vaval, St. Jean, ☎ 29-75-69 The shops are open from 7 am to 7 pm, Monday-Saturday, and from 7 am to 1 pm, Sundays.

Mayas To Go (Centre Commercial, St. Jean) is an offshoot of the gourmet restaurant on Public Beach. The salads are made fresh daily (they vary day-to-day) and there are specialty sandwiches. There is a small gourmet market as well. Open 8 am-10 pm. ☎ 29-83-70.

*Closed
Monday.*

La Route des Boucaniers (Waterfront, Gustavia) is both a restaurant and take-out shop that supplies hot and cold take-out dishes, particularly for those stocking for private yachts and day-sails. The restaurant opens for breakfast at 9 am, with the take-out boutique opening at 10 am. ☎ 27-73-00.

VitOlive (Lorient) specializes in organic and vegetarian food, including sandwiches, tapas, tapenades and olives. Open 10 am-7 pm. No credit cards. ☎ 52-96-22.

Closed Sunday.

Local Watering Holes

Some places take on an aura that is larger than life, especially in a place like the Caribbean where boats and yachts move from island to island. One of those places is **Le Select,** on rue Charles de Gaulle at rue de la France, the busiest corner of Gustavia. Not much to look at, Le Select's reputation draws boat crews, young locals who drop in for a beer and dominoes after work, and just about every visitor to St. Barts, from Rockefellers to Swedish royalty.

Founder and owner Marius Stackelborough, a Swedophile, has portraits of Swedish kings on the walls along with postcards from his friends across the globe and newspaper clippings about Le Select from papers all over the world. The many languages spoken throughout the enclosed bar area make it seem like a Tower of Babel. The crowd usually spills over into the open courtyard shaded by seagrape trees. A must here is the "Cheeseburger in Paradise," named for the Jimmy Buffett song. Jimmy, who is here often, usually entertains. A must-stop. Hours are Monday through Saturday, 10:30 am to 10:30 pm, all year.

Diagonally across the street, the more sedate **Bar de l'Oubli** draws many of the same imbibers as Le Select. It has a more extensive menu and its tables are covered. Better food than Le Select, but not nearly as much fun. Hours are 7:30 am to 1 pm, including Sunday.

La Cave de Saint Barthelemy

French wines are considered the world's finest. **La Cave** imports wines from over 300 vintners and has 300,000 bottles in stock at all times. This warehouse (absolutely functional, not elegant) is climate-controlled to keep the wines at their optimum temperature.

Reds from Bordeaux, Burgundy and the Rhone Valley, whites, and a wide range of champagnes are sold here – by the bottle and the case. They will ship your purchase home for you (subject to duty). If you enjoy fine wines, you'll enjoy visiting La Cave. Hours: Tuesday-Friday, 9 am to noon; 3 to 6 pm. Saturday and Sunday, 10 am to noon. Closed Monday. ☎ 27-63-21; fax 27- 87-05.

After Dark

As previously noted, St. Barts has an unusually large number of restaurants for such a small island. And they don't roll up the "rues" right after dinner the way so many Caribbean islands do. If you want to enjoy a show, dance the night away or listen to jazz at a table with a view, you can.

> ▣ **TIP**
>
> We'll offer some suggestions below, but to find out what's happening when you are on the island, check the daily newspaper, *Le Journal de St. Barth,* and ask your hotel concierge.

Piano Bars

Carl Gustaf (Gustavia) has great views and top-notch pianists. In season a jazz/guitar act takes over. Popular late and at sunset. ☎ 27-82-83.

L'Ananas (Gustavia), in an old restored manor house, has great views and a piano man that stays till 1 am. ☎ 27-63-77.

La Mandala (Gustavia) is right next door. Tapas and drinks served from 5 pm-11 pm. Drinks and music till midnight. ☎ 27-96-96.

Guanahani (Grand Cul de Sac) has a piano in its lobby as well as a cocktail lounge. You can enjoy your drink on the nearby outer terrace as well. ☎ 27-66-60.

Key West Café (Gustavia) sits on the waterfront. It opens at 6 pm for the glorious sunsets and stays open till the wee hours. ☎ 52-02-18.

Le Z51 (La Pointe, Gustavia) is a popular piano bar, but also hosts live concerts that feature guitar and other instruments. ☎ 65-74-81

Manapany Cottages (Anse des Cayes) has its piano bar on the terrace adjacent to the crashing waves. ☎ 27-66-55.

Imbibing, Music, Etc.

Boubou's (El Sereno Hotel, Grand Cul de Sac) sits on the beach, serves a North African menu and is reputed to have St. Barts' best DJs. You can come for drinks and music. ☎ 29-83-01.

Do Brazil (Shell Beach, near Gustavia) is one of the most "in" spots on island. Draws lots of tanned sleek bodies for good Brazilian food, drinks and music. Stays open late. ☎ 29-06-66.

Le Ti St-Barth (Point Milou) bills itself as a Caribbean Tavern, but is best known for its fabulous barbecues. Lovely views of St. Barts' most beautiful residential area. Serves till 11 pm nightly. ☎ 27-97-71.

Tapas Bar (Eden Rock Hotel, St. Jean) has a lovely setting on the hill overlooking the beach. It's a relaxing spot to enjoy late afternoon or early evening drinks, with delicious tapas. ☎ 29-79-99.

American Bar at L'Escale Restaurant (La Pointe) stays open even after the last crust of pizza is gone. Draws a young crowd that plays backgammon and watches music videos. ☎ 27-86-07.

Le Repaire (Gustavia) stops serving at 10:30 but the bar, reggae music and billiard tables keep going till midnight. ☎ 27-72-48.

Le Select and **Bar de L'Oubli** (rue de France, Gustavia) sit on diagonal corners and are both popular hangouts. Le Select draws the beer and burger crowd till 10:30 pm and L'Oubli draws the beer and billiard crowd till 10 pm.

Le Santa Fe (near Gouverneur Beach) has a big screen TV often tuned to US sports events or international soccer matches. ☎ 27-61-04.

Le Pelican (St. Jean) serves Creole food, has a very popular bar and stays open late. There is an open-air terrace on the beach. ☎ 27-70-92.

Dancing (disco)

Feeling (near the Santa Fe Restaurant) is a nightclub with live music for dancing and cabaret shows at midnight. Opens at 10 pm and closes at 2 or 3 am. ☎ 27-88-67.

Le Petit Club (Gustavia) for late night dancing. It opens at 10 pm. ☎ 27-66-33.

La Licorne (Lorient) is very popular with locals. It's open only on Saturdays from 10 pm. ☎ 27-83-94.

Le Deck (Gustavia) serves Italian light foods, with music and dancing nightly from 9 pm. You can come earlier for drinks and finger foods starting at 6:30 pm. ☎ 27-26-07.

Movie Rentals

There is no cinema theater on St. Barts, but it does have several video rental shops and they have current videos in several languages. Many hotels have TVs and VCRs as part of the furnishings. You can be a couch potato.

Tropic Video, St. Jean . . . ☎ 27-98-85
St. Barth Video Club . . . ☎ 27-68-39

St. Barts A To Z

AT&T

To access AT&T Direct Services, ☎ 0800-99-00-11.

Banks

Banque Française Commerciale, rue Charles de Gaulle, Gustavia. ☎ 27-62-62. Saint Jean branch, ☎ 27-65-88. Hours: 8 am to noon and 2 pm to 3:30 pm. Closed weekends, holidays and afternoons preceding holidays.

Doctor On Call

Should you require a physician on a weekend or holiday evening, there is a service to help you from 7 pm to 7 am at ☎ 27-76-03.

Drinking Water

Do not drink tap water. Hotels and restaurants serve filtered water. Bottled water from Guadeloupe and France is sold here.

Electric Current

Voltage is 220 AC 60 cycles. Sockets have two round-prong outlets. US appliances need converters and adapters.

French Wines

See La Cave de Saint Barthelemy, page 114.

Hitchhiking

Hitchhiking is very common on the island.

Hospital

Gustavia Clinic. ☎ 27-60-35.

Language

French is the official language. Some older folks speak to one another in an old Norman dialect. People working in hotels and restaurants and young people in general speak English.

Mini Markets

Closed Sundays. **Mini-Mart & Jojo** in Lorient are open from 7:30 am to noon, and 2 pm to 7 pm.

Monoshop in Marigot is open from 8 am to 1 pm and again from 3 to 7 pm.

Newspaper

Daily, French and English.

NFL Withdrawal

Can't miss Monday night football or the big game on Sunday? Head to the Santa Fe restaurant at Morne Lorne (near Gouverneur Beach) for burgers, brew and football on a big screen TV.

Pharmacies

In Gustavia on Quai de la République. ☎ 27-61-82.

In Saint Jean in La Savane Commercial Centre. ☎ 27-66-61.

Physicians

There are several dentists on the island as well as a pediatrician, an opthamologist and other specialists. Your best bet is to check with the concierge. Villa renters should contact their rental agent.

Post Offices

The island's main post office is on rue de Centenaire in Gustavia. Branches are located in Saint Jean and Lorient. Mail from St. Barts takes two to three weeks to reach the United States.

Religious Services

In Gustavia - Roman Catholic Church on rue du Presbitaire; Anglican Church on rue de Centenaire.

In Lorient - Roman Catholic Church.

In Colombier - Roman Catholic Church.

Check mass times with your concierge.

Special Island Events

Contact the St. Barts Tourist Office for exact dates.

Carnival (pre-Lenten celebration): Costumes, parades and the burning of the Carnival King on Ash Wednesday, usually February.

St. Barts Film Festival: Features Caribbean films in April.

The **Festival Gastronomique** lasts two weeks in April.

The **Classical & Jazz Music Festival** is held in January.

Feast Day of St. Bartholomew & Seafarers Festival takes place in August.

Boubou's St. Barths' Festival, in August, features jazz, reggae and hip-hop, with over 70 musicians and DJs from Europe, South America and the Caribbean.

An **International Art Exhibit** is held in December.

Supermarkets

Match Supermarket (La Savane, St. Jean) is a full-size supermarket, with meats, fish, baked goods and imported frozen and canned foods. Hours: Monday-Thursday, 8 am-1 pm, 3-8 pm; Friday and Saturday, 8 am-8 pm; Sunday, 9 am-1 pm, 4-7 pm. ☎ 27-68-16.

AMC Fleurs, Gustavia Harbor. Monday, Tuesday, Thursday and Friday, 8 am to 7 pm; Wednesday 8 am to 1 pm; Saturday 8 am to 5 pm.

Take-Out Food

See *Picnic Fare* under *Best Places to Eat*, page 112.

Telephones

St. Barts Area Code is 590.

Calls from the US are international. You must dial 011 + 590 + 590 + the number.

It's cheaper and faster to use a calling card for overseas calls.

Calls to French St. Martin are direct dial and require no area code. For calls to Dutch Sint Maarten, you must dial 00-599-54 + the five-digit number.

There are public telephone booths at different points on the island. No coins are accepted. You must purchase a telecarte at the post office (Gustavia, Saint Jean, Lorient). The card can be used for local and international calls. Phone booths can be found in the shopping centers of Saint Jean, Gustavia Port, Corossol, Lorient, Colombier among others.

Time Zone

St. Barts time is one hour ahead of Eastern Standard Time. When it is 6 am in Miami, it is 7 am in St. Barts. The time is the same when the east coast is on daylight savings time. They use a 24-hour clock.

Tourist Offices

In Gustavia on Quai Charles de Gaulle. ☎ 27-87-27. Hours: 8:30 am-6 pm, Monday through Friday; 8:30 am to noon on Saturday.

In New York, contact the **French Tourist Board**, 444 Madison Ave., New York, NY 10022. ☎ 212-838-7800.

The official website is www.saint-barths.com.

Yacht Visitors

Sailboats can anchor in Gustavia, Colombier, Public and Corossol and may pick up provisions at **Loulou's Marine** , ☎ 27-62-74. Another good choice, **La Route des Boucaniers**, ☎ 27-73-00, is nearby on the dock.

Sint Maarten/ Saint Martin

This is the world's smallest land mass that is home to two sovereign nations.

Peter Stuyvesant, who fought here for Holland, would be hard-pressed to find much Dutch culture on the island today. Sint Maarten, with its bustling capital Philipsburg, is a wonderful vacation destination, however. The southern (Dutch) portion of the island has the largest number of duty-free shops in the Caribbean. It has modern high-rise resort hotels, lovely beaches, a golf course, good restaurants and gambling casinos.

The French side of the island has retained more of its French culture, language and tranquility. It has grown more slowly and even its new hotels are low-rise. There are almost as many duty-free shops, but these continue to close at noon for a long leisurely lunch. And what would a slice of France be like without great food? St. Martin rivals nearby St. Barts as the gourmet capital of the Caribbean. While few Dutch people have moved here, a large number of French have emigrated in recent years. Many have opened the restaurants, cafés and bakeries that give the streets of Marigot the same aroma as that of tiny Riviera towns.

But together, the Dutch-French island offers a dynamite vacation, particularly when you add West Indian culture to the mix.

★ NOTE

We use "St. Martin" when referring to the island as a whole. "Sint Maarten" is used specifically for the Dutch side.

The island has 37 stunning beaches, some on the Atlantic and others on the Caribbean. The difference in the waters creates options for every type of watersport. Beach shacks stock top-rated gear for windsurfers, Jet Skiers and boogie boarders. They even give lessons. St. Martin's beaches retain the French tradition of topless bathing. Clothing-optional beaches exist as well. The island's central location makes it easy to take day-trips to Anguilla, Saba, St. Eustatius and St. Barts. Landlubbers can play golf, tennis and sand volleyball or go horseback riding. Hiking trails thread the island. You can pamper yourself with a seaweed massage. There are picturesque West Indian towns to explore and a lively market where you can test your bargaining skills.

After the sun sets you can enjoy a gourmet dinner or a finger lickin' one before you head to a casino or a sidewalk café to listen to calypso or reggae.

Philipsburg, the Dutch capital, and Marigot, the French one, are just 10 miles apart. The island's cultural divisions will increase your enjoyment and broaden your travel horizons even as you get a great suntan.

Getting There

By Air

 International flights from the US and Europe land at **Princess Juliana International Airport** on the island's southern coast (the Dutch side). Major US carriers include **American Airlines**, with non-stop flights from New York (in season) and several direct flights daily through Miami and Puerto Rico (☎ 800-433-7300). **Continental Airlines** and **USAir** are also good choices. Continental Airlines and USAir also connect through Puerto Rico. Major European carriers such as AirFrance, KLM and Lufthansa land at Pointe-à-Pitre Airport in Guadeloupe.

Commuter airlines have flights from Puerto Rico and Guadeloupe. These include:

Air Guadeloupe . . . . . . ☎ 590-87-12-14
American Eagle . . . . . . ☎ 599-545-2040
Winair . . . . ☎ 599-545-4230

There is a small airport, **Espérance Grand Case**, on the French side of Saint Martin. It can handle only commuter-size planes and inter-island flights from Guadeloupe and St. Barts.

> **▣ TIP**
>
> Make the connecting flight reservation at the same time as your long-distance flight.

Entry Requirements

US citizens arriving at Princess Juliana Airport or Espérance Grand Case Airport need either a valid passport, a passport with an expiration date less than five years old, an original birth certificate, or a voter registration card. The latter two also require a photo ID. A return or continuing flight ticket is also required. European Union citizens require a valid passport or a national identity card. French citizens arriving at Espérance from Guadeloupe do not need documents.

No vaccinations are required.

Money Matters

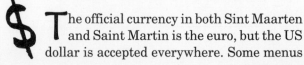

The official currency in both Sint Maarten and Saint Martin is the euro, but the US dollar is accepted everywhere. Some menus on the French side list prices in euros and French francs.

Major credit cards are accepted at hotels, restaurants and shops, as are traveler's checks. Some hotels will require a deposit by check.

Tipping

In lieu of a tip, a 10 to 15% service charge is added to your restaurant bill in both Saint Martin and Sint Maarten. It is customary to leave an additional amount when the service merits it.

Getting Around

Navigating The Island

One major road (the name changes frequently) circles the island, with smaller roads leading from it to the towns and bays. Another major road goes through the island connecting Philipsburg and Marigot. It cuts 15 minutes off the circular route's time.

Car/Jeep Rentals

Most visitors to the island rent a car. Roads are paved and well maintained, and there is very little traffic except on the entrance roads to Philipsburg. Drive on the right side of the road as in the US.

Road signs are easy to read.

International car rental agencies have booths at the airport. There are many local agencies throughout the island and at major hotels.

> **▣ TIP**
>
> Reserve your car in advance in high season. Off-season, you might consider a local rental agency since rates are lower and cars comparable. You can bargain.

Major companies include:

Avis . . . . ☎ 800-331-1084
Budget . . . . ☎ 800-472-3325
Eurocar (National) . . . . ☎ 800-328-4567
Hertz . . . . ☎ 800-654-3131

Local companies on the Dutch side include:

Adventure Car Rental . . . ☎ 599-544-3688
Safari Rentals . . . . ☎ 599-545-3180
Sunshine Car . . . . ☎ 599-545-2684

On the French side:

Espérance Rentals,
Marigot . . . . ☎ 590-87-51-09
Hibiscus Rentals,
Baie Nettlé . . . . ☎ 590-87-74-53

Adventure Car Rental,
Queen Juliana Airport, Marigot, Simpson Bay,
Dockside Marina . . . . ☎ 590-29-23-74

Motorcycle & Scooter Rentals

Harley Davidson . . . . . . ☎ 599-544-2779
Cole Bay (Dutch)

L 2 R . . . . ☎ 590-52-06-72
Baie Nettlé (two locations - French)

⚡ WARNING

Readers have reported violent attempts to steal scooters on the road between Orient Beach and Baie Rouge. Teenagers on another moped have been known to pull alongside and kick the scooter in an effort to cause a loss of control.

Taxis

Taxis display authorization stickers. They meet flights at Princess Juliana and Espérance Airports. There are taxi stands in Philipsburg, Marigot, Grand Case and Maho. Elsewhere, taxis must be called. There is a fee schedule, but there are no meters. Fares go up 25% after 10 pm and 50% after midnight.

In Marigot . . . . ☎ 590-87-56-54
Grand Case Airport . . . . . ☎ 590-87-75-79
In Philipsburg . . . . ☎ 599-542-2359

Buses

There is no public bus system on the island, but private buses run between 7 am and 7 pm. They connect towns with one another but do not go directly to beaches or bays. There are no bus stops. Just stand at the side of the road and flag it down. Very inexpensive.

Inter-Island Travel

By Plane

See Getting There, *page 127, for airlines.*

Small puddle-jumpers connect Sint Maarten with St. Barts. Flights take 15 minutes and are frequent throughout the day. There are also daily flights to Saba and St. Eustatius, but these run less frequently.

Flights from Saint Martin also connect to Saint Barts and Guadeloupe. There is a $10 departure tax.

By Boat

To Anguilla: Ferries leave Marigot dock every half-hour from 8 am to 5:30 pm daily. The trip takes about 20 minutes. You need a passport or other forms of identification listed in *Entry Requirements*, above. There is a $2 departure tax.

Check on current schedules at desk.

To St. Barts: *Voyager* is a ferry service that makes the crossing several times daily. It leaves from Marigot's dock at 9:30 am and 6:30 pm, returning at 7:15 am and 4:30 pm. Check schedules. The trip takes 1½ hours and circles the Dutch coastline before heading out to sea. The return trip takes one hour and circles the northern (French) coast. ☎ 590-87-10-68.

Voyager has open-air and enclosed seating.

Voyager makes the trip to St. Barts from Bobby's Marina in Philipsburg twice weekly. This is more of an excursion than a ferry service. The trip takes one hour. ☎ 599-524-4096 for schedules.

At this writing the adult round-trip fare from Philipsburg is $44. There is a $6 departure tax as well. The $50 fare from Marigot includes the departure tax. Children between the ages of two and 12 pay a third less.

Oyster Lines, leaving from Captain Oliver's Resort Marina in Oyster Bay, has become very popular. It makes the crossing twice daily at 8:30 am and 4 pm, with returns at 9:45 am and 5:15 pm. The trip takes only 45 minutes since their ferries are smaller and faster than *Voyager* and Oyster Bay is St. Martin's easternmost point. The round-trip fare is $48. ☎ 590-87-46-13.

The Edge makes the crossing in under one hour as well. Once again, this is an excursion rather than a ferry service. *The Edge* leaves from Pelican Marina, Simpson Bay (Dutch side). ☎ 544-2640.

The crossing takes one hour.

To Saba: You can plan a day-trip or a longer stay on the lovely Dutch island of Saba. It has quaint villages, a rain forest and terrific scuba diving. *The Edge* (Dutch side) and *Voyager* (French & Dutch side) make the trip twice weekly. Call above numbers for schedules. Round-trip fare is $60, with an additional $30 for lunch and scuba diving.

Orientation

The political division has lasted for 350 years. There is a cultural division as well. The northern part of Saint Martin has retained French traditions and customs. It has the ambience of a town on the French Riviera transported to the West Indies. French is both the official language and the conversational one. It is spoken on the streets and in the hotels, restaurants and shops. In the market you will hear the lilting English common in the Caribbean. French restaurants, cafés and bakeries are important parts of the landscape. Restaurants and shops operate on the European system, closing at midday for a

Above: *Carnival, Sint Maarten.*
Below: *Flamboyant tree.*
(Courtesy of Sint Maarten Tourist Office)

Cupecoy Beach, Sint Maarten.
(Courtesy of Sint Maarten Tourist Office)

Above: *Overlooking Philipsburg, from Fort Amsterdam, Sint Maarten.*
Below: *Guavaberry Shop, Sint Maarten.*
(Both photos courtesy of Sint Maarten Tourist Office)

Above: *Yacht races, Sint Maarten.*
(Courtesy of Sint Maarten Tourist Office)

Below: *Philipsburg, Sint Maarten, at night.*
(Courtesy of Marketur)

Heinecken Regatta race off Sint Maarten.
(Courtesy of Marketur)

Above: *Dr. A.C. Wathey Cruise Port, Sint Maarten.*
Below: *School children during Dutch Carnival.*
(Both photos courtesy of Marketur)

Above: *Diving the reefs, Sint Maarten.*
Below: *West Indies Mall in Marigot.*
(Both photos courtesy of Marketur)

Above: *Esmeralda Hotel, Orient Bay Village.*
Below: *Marketplace, Marigot.*
(Both photos courtesy of French St. Martin Tourist Board)

Above: *Hotel Beach Plaza, Marigot.*
(Courtesy of French St. Martin Tourist Board)

Below: *View from dining room at La Samanna, Baie Longue.*
(Courtesy of Orient-Express Hotels)

Above: *Le Méridien Hotel, Anse Marcel.*
(Courtesy of French St. Martin Tourist Board)

Below: *Pool at Guanahani Hotel, Grand Cul de Sac, St. Barts.*
(Courtesy of Orient-Express Hotels)

Above: *Gustavia, St. Barts.*
(Courtesy of St. Barts Tourist Board)

Below: *Cap Juluca, Anguilla.*
(Courtesy of Marilyn Marx)

Cap Juluca, Anguilla.
(Courtesy of Marilyn Marx)

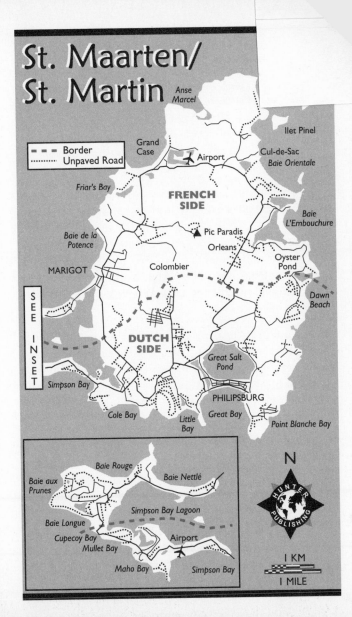

St. Maarten/
St. Martin

Anse Marcel

- - - Border
.... Unpaved Road

Ilet Pinel

Grand Case

Airport

Cul-de-Sac
Baie Orientale

Friar's Bay

FRENCH SIDE

Baie L'Embouchure

Baie de la Potence

Pic Paradis

Orleans

Oyster Pond

MARIGOT

Colombier

SEE INSET

Dawn Beach

DUTCH SIDE

Great Salt Pond

Simpson Bay

PHILIPSBURG

Cole Bay

Little Bay

Great Bay

Point Blanche Bay

Baie Rouge

Baie Nettlé

Baie aux Prunes

Simpson Bay Lagoon

Baie Longue

Cupecoy Bay
Mullet Bay

Airport

Maho Bay

Simpson Bay

N

HUNTER PUBLISHING

1 KM
1 MILE

leisurely lunch. Many shopkeepers and restaurateurs are recent arrivals from France.

⭐ **DID YOU KNOW?**

St. Martin is a sub-prefecture of Guadeloupe (as is St. Barts), and residents vote in both local and French national elections.

To longtime residents, Saint Martin has become very built up, but as a visitor, you won't think so. True, there are many new hotels, but few are large. You'll appreciate the fine restaurants and shops, particularly since Marigot is a duty-free port. The beaches are largely undeveloped, with only a few offering even a watersports center.

Sint Maarten, in the south, rushed headlong into the second half of the 20th century, becoming a tax haven, which allowed foreign investment in its tourist industry. Large resort hotels were constructed almost overnight and casinos flourished, as did duty-free shops. The southern half of the island became a major cruise ship destination.

Sint Maarten's economy boomed. It drew workers from other Caribbean islands, many of whom arrived illegally. Few people speak Dutch, although it is the official language. English is the working language and many residents speak Papiamento (an idiomatic language spoken in the Dutch West Indies). Spanish is common as well. Sint Maarten might have continued to flourish but for Hurricane Luis, which hit the island in September 1995, badly damaging hotels, yachts and homes. Even the airport was closed for two months. Many hotels were closed for a year or more and even now some still remain closed. Money from Holland and other foreign sources was slower in coming here than on the French side. Perhaps it is because Sint Maarten is part of the Netherlands Antilles (with Saba, St. Eustatius, Bonaire and Curaçao) and not an integral part of Holland itself. As such, the Dutch governor is only the titular head of the government. The local legislature is the actual one.

Although a French flavor remains in the north and a Dutch one is still felt in the south, the two have blended and meshed with the West Indian culture over the past 350 years. Hence, local foods, frenetic markets and traditional festivals are celebrated with equal fervor on both sides of the imaginary border.

The political and cultural divisions will not be important to you as you explore the towns, swim at the beaches, shop in the stores or eat in the restaurants. Only casino-hoppers will have to head south.

Sint Maarten/St. Martin

Towns & Sights

Princess Juliana Airport

In Sint Maarten, Princess Juliana handles all international flights and the bulk of inter-island flights as well. On a south coast isthmus, it is five miles west to Marigot and six miles east to Philipsburg.

Philipsburg

The capital of Sint Maarten is built around Great Bay, a sheltered harbor that is the busiest port in the Lesser Antilles. Surprisingly small, the heart of the town is only four streets wide, restricted by the Great Salt Pond just inland. Front Street edges the coast and is the busiest street in town. It is lined with duty-free shops, restaurants of all types, small inns and two casinos. Back Street, the second block, is a less crowded version of Front Street. The streets are connected by narrow alleys called "steegjes," which have shops and nightclubs as well. Philipsburg is bustling during the day and night.

Front Street is "Vorstraat" in Dutch. And Back Street is "Achterstraat."

Simpson Bay Lagoon

This large lagoon is rimmed by narrow isth-
muses. Part of it is Dutch and it is the busiest
watersports center for the south side of the
island. The French side, called Baie Nettlé, has
a series of moderately priced hotels. Simpson
Bay Lagoon's eastern tip forms the Port La Royale Marina in Marigot.

Maho Bay

Adjacent to the airport, the village at Maho Bay
is the heart of Sint Maarten. It has several
resort complexes, good restaurants, two shopping malls and two casinos. Surrounded by
vacation villas, Maho is the local hangout for
Americans. It has a beach strip.

Mullet Bay

The pride of Sint Maarten, Mullet Bay was
dominated by an upscale villa resort built
around the island's only golf course. Badly damaged by Hurricane Luis in 1995, the resort has
never been rebuilt. Only the golf course is in
operation as we go to print. The town centered
around the golf facility looks like a ghost town
with hardly any shops open. Check on progress.
Maho Bay, Mullet Bay and Cupecoy Bay, adjacent to one another, have beach strips.

Just west of Maho.

Sint Maarten/St. Martin

Marigot

La Royale Marina is on the lagoon.

The capital of French Saint Martin is a delightful town with two hubs. The **Port La Royale Marina** is enclosed on three sides by upscale shops, gourmet restaurants and charming cafés. Lots of small sailboats and motorboats anchor here. This is the "French" hub in town. Two blocks away, **Place du Marché** on Marigot Bay is the site of the West Indian flea market, the tourist office, a few upscale French restaurants and a far larger number of moderately priced West Indian eateries where local bands play each night. Ferries leave from the dock for Anguilla and St. Barts. This is the "West Indian" hub in town. **Rue Charles de Gaulle** and **Rue de la République** are the two most important shopping streets in Marigot.

Grand Case

This is a picturesque village with many traditional-style homes and restored Creole mansions that house fine restaurants. **Boulevard Grand Case** is often called the Caribbean's Restaurant Row. Good hotels and a wide crescent-shaped beach are here as well.

Orient Bay

The beach at Orient Bay is the longest on the island. Hurricane Luis made it wider – a giant plus since this clothing-optional beach is crowded with beachfront restaurants, water-sport centers, and even a nudist camp. Topless bathing is the norm on the island, but many people go completely nude here. The hillsides around the bay house hotels and villa communities. The action starts early and ends late.

Terres Basses

This lowland area joins Cupecoy Bay (Dutch) and the beautiful Baie Longue, Baie aux Prunes and Baie Rouge on the French side of the border monument. Many upscale residential communities are here, as is La Samanna, the island's finest resort.

On the western border.

Oyster Pond Bay

A stunning bay that is split by that imaginary border. It has fine resorts on both sides as well as an active marina. The bay is encircled by hills and has only a narrow outlet to the Atlantic. The waters are so calm that it looks like a pond.

On the eastern border.

A Brief History

The island now known as Saint Martin/ Sint Maarten was spotted by Columbus during his second voyage in 1493. The date, November 11, was the Feast Day of St. Martin of Tours, after which the island was named. But Columbus made no attempt to colonize the island. The early inhabitants of the small islands in the Lesser Antilles were peaceful **Arawak Indians**. They were followed by the fierce **Caribs**, another South American tribe that took no prisoners – European or Indian. The Caribs referred to the land mass as "Sualougia," a place to get salt, a resource that proved to be key to its later colonization.

By the 1600s, Spanish, French and Dutch pirates and navies roamed through these waters looting at will. The Dutch took note of the vast salt ponds on the southern shore. They needed salt to preserve the herrings they brought back to Holland, and they claimed the island in 1631, building a fort on the western tip of Great Bay. Nonetheless, the Spanish overran the fort and staked their claim to the island by building a fort on Pointe Blanche, the eastern tip of the bay. During this time, the French staked their claim to the northern part of the island.

In an effort to regain the island, the Dutch attacked from Curaçao (led by Peter

Stuyvesant, then governor of the Dutch possessions). Stuyvesant fought valiantly, but he was
unsuccessful. This was a tiny battle, part of the
80 Years War between Spain and Holland.

★ DID YOU KNOW?

Stuyvesant lost a leg during
this battle, earning him the
nickname Pegleg, a name that
followed him when he became
governor of New Amsterdam,
now New York.

Although victorious, the Spanish decided to
abandon the island and released the Dutch and
French prisoners they held. The prisoners
determined to stay and encouraged colonization by their countrymen. Over the years, nei-
ther side could gain the upperhand and finally
they decided to share the island.

The Great Divide

An island legend says that the French/
Dutch border was set in a walking race. A
Dutchman and a Frenchman stood back to
back and set off in opposite directions to
walk around the island till they met. Appar-
ently, the Dutchman was slower, either because he was fat or he stopped often to drink
gin (take your pick). No matter, the island
was divided, with the French retaining 21
square miles in the north and the Dutch
with 16 square miles in the south.

Sint Maarten/St. Martin

Although the above legend makes for interesting reading, it's more likely that the majority of land was given to the French due to the larger French naval presence in the area. The border has remained firm for 350 years, although claims were made until 1816. The formal border remained unmarked until a commemorative stone was placed there in 1948.

Sugarcane plantations were established on the island in the late 1700s and slaves were brought in to work in the fields and in the houses. Sugar was the sole economic factor on the island, and when slavery was abolished (on the French side in 1848, and on the Dutch side in 1863), the economy collapsed. The former slaves remained on the island and intermarriages created the predominant Creole culture.

In the 1940s, Princess Juliana Airport was built as the Dutch side became a tax haven and duty-free port. Foreign investments in the tourist industry created resort hotels, casinos, and shops almost overnight. Great Bay became the largest port in the Lesser Antilles and the booming economy lured immigrants from nearby islands looking for work. Hurricane Luis in September, 1995, put a major crimp in the economy, resulting in many people being unemployed for long periods of time. Sint Maarten is now part of the Netherlands Antilles, along with Curaçao, Bonaire, Saba and St. Eustatius.

The French side, also a duty-free port, did not encourage foreign investment and thus developed more slowly. The difference in pace remains till this day. St. Martin is part of the French Overseas Department governed through Guadeloupe. Citizens here vote in French national elections as well as local ones.

Sunup to Sundown

When you imagine what your days on St. Martin will be like, think water. The island offers the turquoise waters of the Caribbean, the rolling waves of the Atlantic and a tranquil lagoon as well. Each is a water playground, and the wilder the watersport, the better. Snorkeling, windsurfing, waterskiing, sailing, Jet Skiing, WaveRunning, sportfishing and parasailing are all readily available. There are a score of exciting dive spots nearby and well-organized trips to each. You can take a day-sail to an uninhabited cay nearby for a picnic and snorkeling over a pristine coral reef, or you can spend a day swimming in the waters of nearby Anguilla or St. Barts.

For beachgoers, there are more than 30 beaches on the coves and bays that mark the island's coastline. If the sandy shores were laid end to end they would reach over 10 miles. Some beaches are short patches wedged between rocky cliffs, while others appear endless – velvety white sand dotted with seagrape and palm trees. While the beach at Orient Bay is a blur of activity, the strip at Baie Lounge is tranquil with only a local entrepreneur to sell soft drinks and rent lounge chairs.

Topless bathing is the norm on the French side of the island and Orient Beach is officially clothing-optional. Other beaches are clothing-optional, but not officially. Swimmers on the Dutch side tend to keep their bikinis on.

Golfers might enjoy the 18-hole course ocean-side at Mullet Bay (see page 170).

In recent years, St. Martin has taken steps to preserve its environment. Trails that were used by farmers during the Colonial era have been reclaimed and new trails allowing access to the very top of the island have been added. There are organized hikes. A marine and coastal reserve has been created to protect part of the island's coral reef. A private organization has carved out a seven-acre park that has hiking trails and all kinds of tropical vegetation.

Bridge Alert!

There is one main road that circles the island. At two points there are bridges that are raised for marine traffic. At Simpson Bay, the bridge is raised at 9:30 am, 11, and at 5:30 pm to allow boat access between Simpson Lagoon and the Caribbean Sea. On Sandy Ground Road, the bridge is raised at 9 am, 2:30 and 5:30 pm for access between the lagoon and the Atlantic Ocean near Marigot. Auto traffic is stoppped for 10 minutes each time.

There are two exciting capitals to explore – one bustling and the other laid back. And there are picturesque villages with traditional Creole buildings and gourmet restaurants to visit. There are even museums.

The shopping here is exceptional and duty-free in both capitals. Jewelry, china, imported resort wear, leathers and cameras are all good buys.

You'll be so active that you'll hardly have time to finish the latest thriller.

French-Side Beaches

Since there are beaches on every part of the island, en route to them you'll also be exploring tiny West Indian hamlets with names like Cripple Gate, Pigeon Tree Hill and Colombier.

All beaches on the island are open to the public, even those that house deluxe resorts. There is normally a path to the beach that bypasses the hotel. Some hotels charge a nominal fee for the use of changing facilities and higher fees for lounge chairs and watersports gear. Some hotels do not permit non-guests to use hotel facilities, even for a fee. Undeveloped beaches frequently have locals that rent lounge chairs and umbrellas, and sell cold drinks. Some have "lolos," or beach shacks that sell barbecued chicken, ribs and lobster.

Generally, the beaches on the French side are cleaner and less developed since many coves and bays do not have hotels on them. Virtually every beach on the Dutch side has a high-rise hotel or villa development on it.

> **⚡ WARNING**
>
> Keep in mind that topless bathing is the norm at pools and beaches on the French side and several beaches are clothing-optional. If you are traveling with children, you might like to explain this cultural difference, or you may prefer to avoid these areas.

Orient Bay Beach

On the island's northeast coast, Orient Beach disproves the generalization above. It is a whirlwind of activity both in the water and on the sand. It is crowded and noisy and it is "the place" on the island where the well-tanned and well-toned go to be seen. And seen they are, since this is a clothing-optional beach and many people take the option, particularly at the southern end, which fronts the naturist camp (see *Accommodations*, page 209).

While Hurricane Luis washed sand off many island beaches, it actually widened Orient Beach. Crescent-shaped and over 1½ miles long, the beach has been divided into sections by beachfront restaurants and watersports rental kiosks. These restaurants are popular day and night, and have indoor and outdoor tables. Among them are Bikini Beach (Spanish food), Kakao (pizza), Kon Tiki (French), Coco Beach (international), and Waikiki (French). Each has a parking lot. Beach volleyball and paddleball games are hard fought, and the turquoise water is dotted with windsurfers and sunfloats. You can rent a lounge chair, but will feel comfortable with your own blanket to sit on and a picnic lunch as well. Several hotels and villa resorts are near Orient Bay (see *Accommodations*).

Baie Longue, Baie Aux Prunes & Baie Rouge

A trio of stunning beaches edge the sea on Terres Basses, the lowland area near the French-Dutch border.

Baie Longue (Long Bay), the most westerly of the three, is the longest and arguably the most beautiful beach on the island. The deluxe La Samanna resort is built on the hillside above this beach. The area that fronts the resort has been landscaped but the rest of the beach has only seagrape trees and tropical plants growing untamed. It's a terrific beach for swimming and snorkeling. No food or gear rentals. There is a path from the parking lot.

Look for the road sign to La Samanna.

You can hike from the northern end of Long Bay to Baie Aux Prunes (Plum Beach) by walking around Pointe du Canonner, which juts out into the bay and is the most westerly point on the island. Plum Bay is totally undeveloped, although there are residential communities on the hills surrounding it. This bay gets rolling waves, and young surfers congregate to test their skills at the northern end near Bird's Cliffs. It is so secluded that nude bathing is common. No food or rentals. There's an access trail from the parking lot. Look for the fence.

The main road sign, "Baie Aux Prunes," is quite faded.

Driving east for one mile you'll see the Baie Rouge (Red Beach) turn-off and a sandy parking lot often filled with mini-vans just beyond it. This is the most popular beach for local tour operators. "David's Hole," at the northern end, is a popular snorkeling spot and it has an interesting coral reef. There are food and lounge chair rental kiosks, but picnic food would probably be your best bet.

Cul De Sac, The Cays & Off-Shore Islands

Le Pinel Restaurant is an informal stop for dinner in Cul de Sac.

Cul de Sac is not the most beautiful beach on the island but it is at the heart of the marine reserve and serves as the kick-off point for boat rides to offshore islands and secluded surfing beaches reached by a coastal trail. Cul de Sac's turquoise waters often have fishing boats bobbing in them. The catch of the day comes in very

early. Nearby, you'll see kite and m
flyers gather on the dark sand be
for one of the wooden boats that m
to Ilet Pinel in five minutes. Uninhabi
a pristine coral reef and two beach shacks tha
serve food and drink. There is a watersports
center for gear rentals as well. Bigger boats
make the run to Tintamarre Island, which has
excellent snorkeling and scuba diving. A
deserted airstrip is right off the beach and
you'll see goats and turtles. Organized scuba
trips come to Tintamarre.

Grand Case Beach

If taking a leisurely swim or a jog along the
beach works up your appetite then head to
Grand Case Beach. Not only are there a dozen
gourmet eateries overlooking the shore, but
directly facing the sand are the best "lolos" on
the island. These beach shacks (now much sturdier) serve the best barbecued ribs, chicken and
lobster you've ever eaten. They are inexpensive
too.

Many "lolos" were destroyed by Hurricane Luis and not rebuilt.

Baie De L'Embouchure & Plage Du Galion

These secluded beaches share a cove within the
marine reserve. The government has established mooring sites here to avoid damage to

the cove's pristine coral reef. The tree-lined arc at L'Embouchure (Coconut Grove), preferred by surfers and snorkelers, has food and water-sports rental shacks. At the northern end of the cove, Galion Beach is barely developed. Its waters are protected by the offshore reef, making the waters calm enough for young children. There is a watersports center here..

road to this ⸱e is unpaved ⸱ut easy to navigate.

Other French-Side Beaches

Friar's Beach sits between Marigot and Grand Case. Good snorkeling beach with "lolos." Look for "La Savanne" turn-off.

Anse Marcel: Calm waters that front Le Méridien Hotel and Marina. Hotel permits rentals of lounge chairs and gear. Restaurant at the beach.

Baie Nettlé: There is an ocean-side beach and a bay-side beach on the isthmus connecting Marigot and Terres Basses. Lots of moderately priced hotels here.

Dutch-Side Beaches
Dawn Beach-Oyster Pond

The paved road to Dawn Beach and Oyster Pond resembles a roller coaster and the beaches are worth every pothole. Dawn Beach is stunning, surrounded by mountains, and many consider it the best snorkeling beach on the island. Refreshments and rentals. Oyster Pond has only a small beach that lures surfers. It also has a marina.

Hermit crab races held here.

TIP

Mrs. B's rents beach chairs and water sports gear and serves great ribs. **Scavengers**, also at Dawn Beach, is the island's expat watering hole.

Cupecoy Beach

Cupecoy looks like the beach on picture postcards. Lined with sandstone cliffs, it has several small coves. Follow the footpaths that connect them. Some are very secluded; many are clothing-optional. Many gay locals and visitors head here as well. Good snorkeling and surfing when the wind is up. Refreshments and rentals.

Maho & Mullet Bays

Maho Beach is long and has deep white sand. It can get crowded because Maho Beach Hotel has 600 rooms. The roar in your ears is not the water but the airplanes landing at Princess Juliana Airport adjacent to the beach. You can easily walk to Mullet Bay. This is a palm-lined strip that fronts the golf course and the villas that were destroyed by Hurricane Luis. Lots of surfers.

Simpson Bay & Lagoon

Simpson Bay is home to a small group of fisher-men that live in traditional Creole *cases* (houses). There are also several resort hotels. The lagoon is the busiest watersports center on the Dutch side of the island. Waterskiing, wind-surfing, Jet Skiing and sailing are only a few of the options. Lots of watersports rentals and food.

Other Dutch-Side Beaches

Great Bay: On the western edge of Philips-burg, Great Bay beach has calm waters and watersports rentals. Windsurfing is very popu-lar.

Near Fort Amsterdam

Little Bay: At the tip of the western peninsula and fronting the Divi Little Bay Resort, this is a narrow strip but good for swimming.

Sights

Philipsburg

This early settlement on Sint Maarten's southern coast became the capital of the Dutch colony in 1733. Led by Scotsman John Philips, the settlement was perfectly situated between a large protected harbor (Great Bay) and a vast saltern (Great Salt Pond). It was the saltern that provided the impetus for the settlement (the Dutch needed salt to preserve the fish they carried back to Holland). The town was built on a sandy strip parallel to the bay.

The saltern, in use till 1949, is home to herons and migrating birds and is partly filled in. Its location has restricted the growth of Philipsburg, so the heart of the city is less than a half-dozen streets wide. Two of those streets, **Front Street** (Vorstraat) and **Back Street** (Achterstraat), run parallel to the bay and the small alleys that connect them (steegjes); they are commercial centers with fine boutiques offering goods at duty-free prices.

Philipsburg, although damaged by several hurricanes, has managed to retain its Colonial Dutch and West Indian architecture. Many of the shops are located in renovated Colonial buildings painted in typical pastels and with gingerbread (fretwork) designs on the wooden eaves, porches and rooftops. One of the best

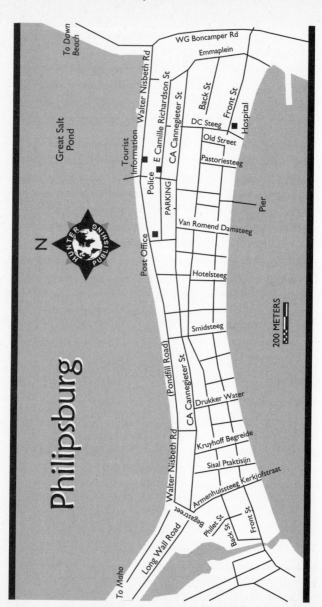

examples of Colonial architecture is the **Pasasgrahan Inn**, on the east end of Front Street. The oldest inn on the island, it was once a royal guest house that hosted Queen Wilhelmina when she visited the island. The most famous building in town is **The Courthouse**, on Front Street at Wathey Square, where the dinghies from cruise ships in the harbor drop and pick up passengers. The white and green building dates to 1793. Renovated several times, most recently in 1994, the building has served as the local council hall, a weigh station, post office, jail and fire station. Today it functions as the court.

Another interesting stop, the **Simartin Museum**, opened in 1989. It provides a historical and geological record of the island and its people. The small museum has a permanent collection, changing exhibits and beautiful antique maps. #7 Spectgjens Arcade. ☎ 24917. Small entrance fee. Hours: Monday through Saturday, 10 am to 4 pm.

Even if you aren't a shopper, you should walk along **Old Street**, a gated street filled with shops that connects Front and Back Streets.

Two forts built in the Colonial period are on the peninsulas guarding Great Bay. On the west, **Fort Amsterdam**, built in 1631, is the oldest Dutch fort in the Caribbean. In spite of its strategic position, commanding the harbor, the fort was captured by the Spanish two years later. The Dutch, led by Peter Stuyvesant, tried

The fort is near the tennis courts at the Divi Resort.

unsuccesfully to recapture it. It was here that Stuyvesant lost a leg before he went on to became governor of New Amsterdam (now New York). Fort Amsterdam stands on Little Bay Peninsula, a 20-minute walk from Front Street. Ruins of the **Spanish-built fort** are visible on Pointe Blanche on the eastern shore of the bay.

Marigot

Philipsburg is a typical West Indian town much like Charlotte Amalie in St. Thomas. Marigot, on the other hand, is more like a town on the French Riviera transplanted to the Caribbean. It was not so long ago that Marigot was a sleepy fishing village, but it has renovated its lovely old houses and put chic duty-free shops in some of them. Its marina, **Port La Royale**, is a handsome complex that comes alive each morning with schooners unloading produce for the market and visitors boarding sailboats for a day of diving. The streets are filled with sidewalk cafés and the aroma of baking baguettes, warm croissants and café au lait. Many people speak French; others, the lilting Caribbean English.

"Marigot" is a French West Indian word meaning "swampy lowland."

Located on the island's western shore, the French selected the townsite because of the large bay encircled by hills that offer protection from the winds. But what is now Marigot Bay looked more like a swamp then, hence the name "Marigot," which in French means a "lowland

Sint Maarten/St. Martin

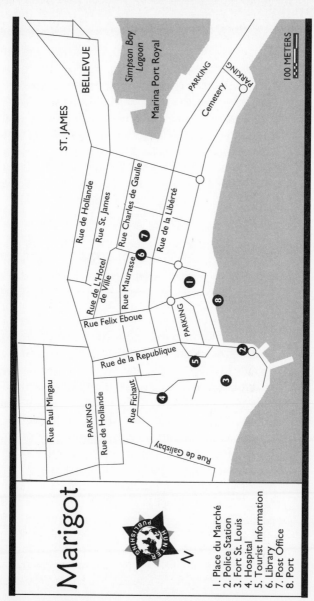

Marigot

HUNTER PUBLISHING

N

1. Place du Marché
2. Police Station
3. Fort St. Louis
4. Hospital
5. Tourist Information
6. Library
7. Post Office
8. Port

subject to flooding." Almost immediately the colony was under attack by the English from nearby Anguilla. The French decided to build a fort, **St. Louis,** on a hill commanding the harbor. Although the British did manage to overrun the fort and settlement, gradually the attacks stopped. The fort was abandoned but has recently been restored and is an interesting spot to visit if only for the fantastic views. It's a 10-minute hike from the dock. The views are great. (You can also drive to Fort St. Louis.)

Marigot has expanded rapidly and, much to the regret of old-timers, the area near Fort St. Louis and north of the dock has several new residential communities and even a US-style shopping center. But these areas are of little interest to visitors.

It's the downtown area that has all the energy, bordered by Port La Royale Marina (south) to rue de la République (north) and the harbor walk of rue de la Liberté, the dock and market square (west) and rue de Hollande (east) that is the main road to Grand Case. Bursting at the seams with places to eat and party, scores of shops that sell designer duds, jewelry, perfumes and wines, Marigot's small streets are its lure. Don't miss the **market**, in operation daily. At the dock, its kiosks are filled with fruits and vegetables, fish, clothing and handicrafts. It's a slice of life on Saint Martin and it isn't strictly for tourists.

History buffs will enjoy the **Musée de Saint Martin**, often called "On the Trail of the Arawaks." Set in a two-story building, it details the island's history from pre-Columbian times to the present. It has pottery, old maps and photos, descriptions of burial sites and practices, and other interesting exhibits. Everything is described in both English and French. The second floor is an art gallery with works by local artists and monthly exhibits. The museum works with the Hope Estate, a dig that seeks to discover early artifacts. Entrance fee. Hours: 9 am to 1 pm and 3 to 7 pm. Closed Sundays. ☎ 590-29-22-84. Near the marina on Sandy Ground Road.

Grand Case

French Saint Martin and Saint Barts vie for "the best dining in the Caribbean" title. Inexplicably, it is this tiny fishing village on the island's northwestern shore that has the "hottest" restaurants on this island. Its main street runs for one mile and has scores of top-notch restaurants. With European-trained chefs in their kitchens, they serve French, Creole, Italian, Vietnamese and Indonesian dishes in elegant surroundings. Many are housed in restored Creole houses, which give the town a quaint, picturesque appeal. The gourmet restaurants are joined by the famed "lolos," beach shacks, where local cooks serve fabulous barbecued chicken, ribs and lobster, and such Caribbean specialties as plantains, rice and peas, and johnnycakes. On alternating Saturdays year-round you can stand on Grand Case Beach and watch sailing races between local fishermen in old fishing boats and their friendly Anguillan rivals. Anguilla is visible on the horizon. Espérance Airport, which has inter-island flights, is near town as well.

Colombier & Orleans

For a peek at what St. Martin looked like 50 years ago, head to Colombier, a tiny hamlet between Marigot and Grand Case and Orleans, farther to the north. Colombier is pastoral, with goats and cows grazing behind old stone walls. Its one street is lined with typical Creole houses, surrounded by flowering gardens and painted in a variety of pastel shades. You can pick up the Sentier des Crêtes hiking trail to Paradise Peak from here as well as from Orléans, another traditional hamlet that was the site of the first French settlement on the island.

Paradise Peak (Pic Paradis)

Standing just under 1,500 feet high, this is the island's highest and greenest point. Moisture-laden clouds must drop their rain here to cross this range, so the area is enveloped in tropical growth. Views are stunning and include both

Marigot and Philipsburg and the nearby islands of St. Barts, Anguilla, Saba and St. Eustatius. The hiking trail to the peak heads north from Colombier or south from Orleans. You can also drive most of the way up. Look for the turn-off between Marigot and Grand Case. Contact **Action Nature** for trail maps, ☎ 590-87-97-87, or the **Dutch Hiking Club**, ☎ 599-542-4917.

Butterfly Farm

Kids will love this landscaped garden, covered with netting, that is home to over 600 butterfly species. You can visit between 9 am and 5 pm daily. The farm is on Galion Beach Road. Don't forget your camera. There are fish ponds, turtles, iguanas and birds as well. ☎ 590-87-31-21.

Sint Maarten Zoo

North of the Great Salt Pond, this small three-acre zoo houses over 60 species of rare and endangered animals and birds native to the Caribbean and South America. Hurricane damage and a lack of funds contributed to the decline of this once-attractive stop. Happily, a private foundation has taken over management of the zoo and is working hard to modernize and make it an animal- and visitor-friendly environment again.

Sint Maarten/St. Martin

Madame Estate is a growing residential area near Philipsburg and offers another slice of Sint Maarten life.

The reptile collection and walk-through aviaries are highlights. On Arch Road, Madame Estate. Hours: Monday through Friday, 9 am to 5 pm; weekends, 10 am to 6 pm.

The Old House Museum

History buffs will enjoy a visit to "The Old House," which has been restored. There is a collection of photos and artifacts that explore life on an 18th-century sugar plantation, the history of the Caribbean and the rum trade. Open daily, 9 am-4 pm. Small entrance fee. Orleans Quarter, ☎ 590-87-32-67.

Water-Based Sports

 Day-sails and snorkeling at nearby islands, scuba dives for beginners and experts, deep-sea fishing and windsurfing – all are well organized here. Check your hotel watersports center and the highly regarded operators below.

Scuba Shop . . . . ☎ 590-87-48-01
Captain Oliver's, Oyster Pond (French)

Octoplus . . . . ☎ 590-87-48-01
Captain Oliver's, Oyster Pond (French)

Scuba Fun Caraïbes . . . . ☎ 590-87-36-13
Anse Marcel (French)

Blue Ocean Divers . . . . . ☎ 590-87-89-73
Nettlé Bay (French)

Aqua Mania . . . . ☎ 599-544-2640
Pelican Marina (Dutch)

Scuba Fun Dive Center . . ☎ 599-542-2333
Divi Little Bay Resort (Dutch)

Leeward Island Divers . . ☎ 599-544-3320
Simpson Bay (Dutch)

Ocean Explorers . . . . . . ☎ 599-544-5252
Simpson Bay (Dutch)

Scuba Diving

There are over 30 dive sites near St. Martin in both the Atlantic and the Caribbean. The water averages 70☐F year-round, and the visibility is excellent. There are not many deep drop-offs, but there are several wrecks and pristine coral reefs with marine life to explore. There are no organized beach dives. Night dives and expert instruction is available if you're looking for certification.

The wreck of the 133-foot British frigate *Proselyte* is the most popular dive here. Near Fort Amsterdam, it sank in 1801. It is visible from the surface, so snorkelers can enjoy it, too. **Hens and Rocks**, off Pointe Blanche, with one large rock and two small ones, is also popular. It has a 70-foot drop-off. **Tintamarre Island**, off the coast near French Cul de Sac, has diving in its sheltered coves.

Watersports Rentals

Chances are that your hotel's waterfront rental center will have the equipment you want, but there are some centers that are outstanding and they are on the beaches where the equipment can be put to maximum use. Rental gear includes Jet Skis, WaveRunners, waterskis, skurf kneeboards, Big Bananas, canoes, kayaks, pedalboats, paddleboats, boogie boards, surfboards and fun boards.

On the French side, contact:

Club Orient Watersports . ☎ 590-87-33-85
Orient Bay

Meridian Watersports. . . ☎ 590-87-67-90
Anse Marcel

Academy de la Glisse . . . ☎ 590-87-99-62
Baie Nettlé

Tropical Wave . . . . ☎ 590-87-37-25
Galion Beach

Grand Case Beach Club. . ☎ 590-87-51-87
Grand Case

On the Dutch side of the island, try:

Pelican Watersports . . . ☎ 599-544-2640
Simpson Bay

Westport Watersports. . . ☎ 599-544-2557
Simpson Bay

Port de Plaisance . . . . . ☎ 599-544-3033
Simpson

Windsurfing

Extremely popular on the island. Simon Windsurfing Club on Or gives lessons. ☎ 590-87-48-16. Also try:

Blue Ocean, Nettlé Bay. . . ☎ 590-87-89-73

Tropical Wave . . . . ☎ 590-87-37-25
Galion Beach

Funny Blue Bubble . . . . ☎ 590-29-55-29
Grand Cul de Sac

Snorkeling & Day-Sails

If you have your own snorkel gear you can head to island beaches with near-shore reefs to enjoy the coral and marine life. Snorkel gear is easy to rent. Beaches with good snorkeling include Dawn Beach, Mullet Bay Beach, Plum Beach, Simpson Bay, Orient Beach and Pinel Island near Grand Cul de Sac.

Snorkeling is often combined with a relaxing day-sail to an uninhabited cay nearby (half-day) or to St. Barts and Anguilla (full day).

Random Wind. . . . . ☎ 599-544-5148
www.randomwind.com

Sand Dollar. . . . . ☎ 599-544-2640
Pelican Marina

Scuba Fun. . . . . ☎ 599-542-2333
Divi Little Bay

Aqua Mania . . . . ☎ 599-544-2640
Pelican Marina

Scoobidoo . . . . ☎ 590-52-02-53
www.scoobidoo.com, Grand Case

Blue Ocean . . . . ☎ 590-87-89-73
Nettlé Bay

Octoplus . . . . ☎ 590-87-20-62
Grand Case

Méridien Watersports . . . ☎ 590-87-67-90
Anse Marcel

Yacht Charters/Boat Rentals

The Moorings . . . . ☎ 800-521-1126
Captain Oliver's, Oyster Pond

Sun Yacht Charters . . . . ☎ 590-87-30-49
Simpson Bay Yacht Club

Sunsail, Oyster Pond . . . . ☎ 800-327-2276

Naytor's Swan Charters . ☎ 590-87-35-48
Anse Marcel

*Make arrange-
ments long
before your arri-
val.*

Deep-Sea Fishing

Captained charters go out for half a day, a full
day or longer. Dolphin, kingfish, sailfish, blue
marlin, tuna and wahoo are the catches.

Black Fin . . . . ☎ 599-547-0210
Great Bay

Lee Deep Sea Fishing . . . ☎ 599-544-4233
Simpson Bay

Deep Sea Fishing . . . . . ☎ 590-87-86-83
Sandy Ground

Marco Sea Dream . . . . . ☎ 590-27-40-95
Anse Marcel

Jet Skiing/Parasailing/Sailing

Kon Tiki Watersports . . . ☎ 590-87-46-89
Orient Beach

Bikini Watersports . . . . ☎ 590-27-07-48
Orient Beach

Jet Sensation Caraïbes . . ☎ 590-23-28-62
Nettlé Bay

Pelican Watersports. . . . . ☎ 599-544-2640
Simpson Bay

Boo Boo Jam Parasail. . . ☎ 590-56-99-01
Orient Bay

Seaworld Explorer

If you don't scuba dive, you can still explore the stunning coral reefs and unusual marine life in the waters near St. Martin. The *SeaWorld Explorer* is an advanced glass-bottom boat. The lower level is submerged so you can see the underwater world through large glass windows. It's fun for children because staff members dive nearby and feed the fish and eels to draw them toward the *Explorer*. It is air-conditioned and the talks are in English. *Seaworld Explorer* leaves daily from Grand Case Pier. Fee: $30 adults, $20 children ages two-12. ☎ 599-542-4078.

Land-Based Sports

Golf

Trees and greens damaged by salt have regenerated.

Mullet Bay Resort's 18-hole golf course, built around a lagoon and near the Caribbean, has continued to operate, although the resort has not reopened since Hurricane Luis. Greens fees are $88. Cart and club rentals are available. ☎ 599-543-2801, ext. 1850.

Horseback Riding

The island offers trail rides for beginners to experienced riders along beaches and off the beaten track. Lessons given. There are champagne rides for two, as well as full moon beach rides.

Caid & Isa, Anse Marcel . . ☎ 590-87-45-70
OK Corral, Oyster Pond . . ☎ 590-61-08-97
Bayside Riding Club. . . . ☎ 590-87-36-64
(between Orient Bay & Galion Beach
Lucky Stables, Cole Bay . . ☎ 599-555-5255

Mountain Biking

Popular for pleasure and for competition. Mountain biking clubs exist and they organize group rides. Near Marigot, the Pass Partout Club and, near Princess Juliana Airport, the Friendly Mountain Biking Association organize races and rides. Contact for clubs and rentals:

Authentic French Tours . ☎ 590-87-05-11

Frog Legs Cyclery (rentals) ☎ 590-87-05-11

Tri-Sport. . . . . ☎ 599-545-4384

Fitness & Spa Services

Many of the larger hotels have fitness centers with treadmills, Lifecycles and Nautilus machines. If yours does not, head to:

Elysées Spa, La Samanna Hotel, ☎ 590-87-64-00. Open to the public by appointment, the spa has expanded twice to meet the growing demand for services. It offers nail and hair care, waxing, plus a half-dozen facials and massages. Body treatments (such as salt scrubs) and "age-reduction" skincare are also available. Prices are comparable to upscale day-spas stateside.

Princess Port de Plaisance Health Club & Spa, ☎ 599-544-3033. Similar in style to the Elysées (recently renovated), there is a beauty salon as well as anti-aging and beauty treatments. Seaweed wraps and aromatherapy treatments are popular. The adjacent health club and seven tennis courts are terrific, and there are lots of fitness classes.

Tennis, Racquetball & Squash

There are tennis courts at many hotels, but squash and racquetball courts are found only at two neighboring hotels in Anse Marcel. **Le Panoramic Privilège Hotel and Spa** welcomes non-guests (☎ 590-87-38-38), as does **Le Méridien Hotel** (☎ 590-87-67-00). Fees vary and are usually charged by the hour. Other choices for tennis:

Guests have priority.

French

Hotel Mont Vernon . . . . ☎ 590-87-62-00
Hotel Laguna Beach . . . . ☎ 590-87-91-75
Hotel Mercure Simpson Beach
. . . . ☎ 590-87-54-54
Nettlé Bay Beach Club . . ☎ 590-87-68-68

Dutch

Princess Port de Plaisance ☎ 599-544-3033
Great Bay Beach Hotel . . ☎ 599-542-2446
Little Bay Beach Resort . ☎ 599-542-2333
Maho Beach Hotel . . . . . ☎ 599-545-2115
Oyster Bay Beach Resort . ☎ 599-543-6040
Pelican Resort & Casino . ☎ 599-544-2503

Hiking

Abandoned to goats and sheep for many years, more than 25 miles of hiking trails cross the island from side to side, leading to stunning viewpoints that offer an upclose look at mango trees, corossol trees, ancient plantation ruins and tiny humming-birds. All the trails, which have been redefined or newly created, are marked. You can hike to Paradise Peak, the highest point on the island.

> ### ▣ TIP
> If you plan to do any hiking, you'll need sturdy shoes, a hat and lots of drinking water.

For hiking trail maps, contact:
Action Nature. . . . . ☎ 590-87-97-87
Dutch Hiking Club . . . . . ☎ 599-542-4917

For group hikes:
Fun Raid Tour . . . . ☎ 590-87-59-24
Heritage Foundation . . . ☎ 599-547-3485
Rising Sun Tours . . . . . ☎ 590-87-14-22

Loterie Farm

Just off the main road to Paradise Peak, Loterie Farm is the place to discover what life was like on an old plantation. You'll see tall avocado and mango trees, as well as all kinds of flora and fauna. Light meals are served at the old farmhouse and there are workshops in yoga and meditation, as well as music sessions. The kids will enjoy the animal petting area and horseback rides. One path leads to Paradise Peak. ☎ 590-87-86-16 for information on special events.

Beach Volleyball

You think Karch Karai takes this game seriously. Wait till you see the game here! Big time games on Friar's Beach, Orient Beach, Galion Beach, Great Bay Beach and Mullet Bay Beach.

St. Martin Beach Volleyball ☎ 590-87-79-73

Shop Till You Drop

Island T-shirts hit the shopping nail right on the head. One says, "Not all treasure on St. Martin is buried" and another, "My daughter went to St. Martin and all I got was a 14k gold ring with an oval sapphire surrounded by diamonds." Need we say more?

For many visitors to the island, shopping is as big a lure as the sun and sand. If you like to shop, you won't be disappointed. Front Street in Philipsburg has more stores than Charlotte Amalie in St. Thomas, and there are also fine shops in Marigot and in Maho Bay Village. Over 500 establishments, along with flea markets and art galleries, are scattered throughout the island. You'll find all of the usual outlets familiar to Caribbean shoppers – Little Switzerland, Colombian Emeralds, Boolchands and Sparkys – but the political division has made for unique specialties. Dutch-side shops feature blue and white Delftware, Edam and Gouda cheeses and sausages, pea soup and Dutch beer. Those on the French side counter with French porcelain, Brie and Camembert cheeses and French wines and perfumes. You'll find many of the same shops in all three locations. Generally, Marigot's shops feature more designer fashions and resortwear and those in Philipsburg have more cameras and electronics.

Best buys include jewelry, watches, crystal, cameras, cigars, flatware, linens, leathers and fine fashions.

> **▣ TIP**
>
> If you are planning to buy cameras, watches or electronic equipment, check prices before leaving home. Some camera/electronic shops give "discounts" if you pay cash.

Since all the shops in Philipsburg are on or near Front Street, it can get very crowded if there are cruise ships in the harbor. Marigot has shops in several locations and far fewer passengers shop there.

Shopping Tips

◎ Shops in both Marigot and Philipsburg list prices in euros. US dollars are accepted everywhere. Major credit cards and traveler's checks are accepted in shops, but not at the market.

🌀 Salespeople do speak English but those in Saint Martin are often less fluent.

🌀 The island is a duty-free port. Prices average 25% less than in the US.

★ DID YOU KNOW?

Guavaberry liqueur, formerly made at home, is now sold in island shops. Guavaberries (not guavas) are indigenous to St. Martin.

Shopping Hours

Shopping hours vary but generally shops in Philipsburg open at 9 am and close at 6 pm, Monday through Saturday. Those in Maho Village stay open till 11 pm. Shops in Saint Martin are open from 9:30 am to 12:30 pm and 3 until 7 pm, Monday through Saturday. Generally closed on Sunday, shops on both sides will open if several cruise ships are expected.

Customs Regulations

US citizens, regardless of age, who have been out of the country for 48 hours and have not used their duty-free allowance within 30 days, are entitled to a $600 duty-free tax exemption. Families traveling together can pool their exemptions. One quart of liquor can be included in the exemption for those over 21.

Canadian citizens who have been out of the country for seven days are permitted a duty-free exemption of $500 Canadian, and $200 Canadian for those out of the country for 48 hours. Exemptions may not be pooled.

Philipsburg

Front Street & Old Street

Front Street, running parallel to the harbor, is lined with shops on both sides. Old Street, at the eastern end of Front Street, is gated and closed to traffic. It has very nice shops.

Oro del Sol Jewelers. One of Front Street's most attractive shops, it stocks such fine watches as Gucci, Ebel, Chopard and Bulgari, along with Van Cleef and Arpels jewelry. They also sell perfumes for men and women, designer sunglasses and Fendi leather goods.

Carat Jewelers. They have several shops on Front Street. One is a watch boutique that sell Breitling, Omega, David Yurman and Franck Muller, among others. You will also find Montblanc and other fine pens and European crystal.

Little Switzerland. This "department store" has mini-boutiques selling fine china, crystal, figurines, fragrances and leather. It is the exclusive island distributor for Rolex watches and also sells Omega, Cartier and Raymond Weil. Rosenthal, Wedgewood, Orrefors and Lladro are among their other specialties.

Boolchands specializes in electronics and cameras; you'll find Aiwa, Sony, Panasonic, Bose, Nikon, Minolta and Pentax, among other well-known brands.

Liz Claiborne. A boutique that features resortwear and sport clothes.

Old Street. **Amazone**. Ladies' clothing, featuring the animale label.

Old Street. **Belgian Chocolate Shop**. You can watch the chocolates being made and buy by the piece or packaged.

Old Street. **Art Deco**. A gift shop that sells bowls and vases made from dried seeds, traditional island dolls, tablecloths and beach gear.

Polo Ralph Lauren has a mini-mall on Front Street. It combines his clothing store with other shops and restaurants.

Endless Summer has swimwear, from bikinis to full-figured styles, from Gottex, Gideon Oberson and others.

Dalila. Indonesian Batik cloth in original designs made into cruisewear, including pareos. Wood carvings and wall hangings, too. *Also in Marigot.*

Shipwreck Shop. Caribbean handicrafts, including wood carvings, baskets, island spices, jellies and cookbooks. *Also in Marigot.*

Last Mango in Paradise. Sells name-brand beach and resortwear. Original T-shirts, dock shoes and accessories. Names like Oakley, Baja Blues and Jams, among others.

Dutch Delfts Blue Gallery sells handpainted Dutch porcelain in the traditional blue and white design, as well as the newer Imari line, which has roots in ancient Japan. All items are imported and come with a certificate of authenticity.

Lipstick offers all the most popular fragrances, cosmetics and skin care products, including Shiseido, Boucheron, Oscar de la Renta and scores of others. *Also in Marigot.*

Goldfinger. A large jewelry store that also stocks fine watches, such as Movado, Piaget, Corum, Esquire and Concord. *Also in Marigot.*

Gold Mine. The exclusive agent for Tiffany jewelry and gifts. Fine watches, including Hublot, Carrera and Carrera, Patek Philippe and Breitling Chronomats.

Sint Maarten Guavaberry company. Sells the island's guavaberry liqueur and other island crafts.

Tommy Hilfiger. A boutique that sells clothing designed by Hilfiger.

Rams. A good choice for duty-free liquors and fine cigars.

Little Europe Jewelers. Carries Hummel and Lladro figurines.

Penha. Has two stores side-by-side that sell clothing and accessories.

Marigot

Marigot shops are near the **Port La Royale Marina**, on Boulevard de France (Harbor Front), and on **rue de la République, rue de la Liberté** and **rue Charles de Gaulle**. Many more shops here sell designer clothing and accessories. Some shops are branches of Philipsburg stores.

West Indies Shopping Mall. Make your first stop at this mall that is adjacent to the dock. Unique for the Caribbean, it is a glass-roofed, air-conditioned, tri-level mall with two-dozen shops, eating spots and a piano bar. Children's clothing, imported ladies' resort wear, French soaps and lotions and gifts. Check out the Lord and Hunter shop. They sell spices, sauces, housewares and cookbooks.

Plaza Caraïbes. Houses a cluster of upscale boutiques, including Hermes (silks and leathers), Ralph Lauren (Polo sportswear), Lipstick (perfumes, lotions), Passions (jewelry) and Avenida Montaigne (leathers, designer clothes).

Rue Charles de Gaulle.

Oro del Sol. A beautifully designed shop with several boutiques. The main shop sells jewelry, including Hublot, Mikimoto, Bulgari and Ebel. The Cartier boutique sells the famed watches and gift items. A third boutique has extensive collections of Baccarat and Lalique crystal, Christofle flatware and Villeroy and Boch china. Still another sells Mont Blanc pens and leather desk sets and daily organizers.

République and Liberté.

European Jewelers. Authentic Italian gold and stone jewelry that is specifically hand-crafted for the shop, as well as famous Swiss timepieces by Cyma, Tabbah and Jean Lasalle.

Rue Charles de Gaulle.

La Romana. Ladies' fashions, including lingerie and swimwear and leather goods from Fendi and Moschino.

République.

Colombian Emeralds. Specializes in gold jewelry and particularly items set with emeralds. A new line of jewelry called "Sea Treasures" is moderate in price. Fine watches too.

République.

O Soleil. Gift items and home accessories imported from southern France. Placemats, tea

Marina.

cozies, tablecloths and wall hangings are just a few of the items available.

Marina.

Plata del Sol. Gift items from Latin America, including silver jewelry from Mexico, pottery from Ecuador, Panama hats and carved balsa woods.

Rue Charles de Gaulle.

Escale Boubou. It's hard to walk around this small shop because items are displayed on the floors, the tables, the walls and even hung from the ceilings. An eclectic mix of African woodcarvings, wood and resin desk ornaments, fragrances and straw items.

Marina.

Banana Moon. Bikinis and beachwear.

République.

Maneks. Electronics, liquors, cigars.

Harborfront.

Ambience Jewelers. Jewelry, Fendi bags.

Harborfront.

Oro del Sol Perfumes. This newest shop sells perfumes from Armani, Kenzo and Guerlain, and cosmetics such as Givenchy, La Prairie and Clinique.

Kennedy.

Fashion Optic. Prada, Chloe, Fred and other designer sunglasses, among others.

Liberté.

Davidoff Boutique. Cigars and smoking accessories.

Kennedy.

Max Mara. Ladies' clothing and accessories.

W.I. Mall & Marina.

L' Occitane. Soaps, candles and other fine aromatic toiletries.

Rue Low Town.

Vinissimo. Wines (French) and spirits.

Reggae Vibes and Souvenirs. Music, crafts, T-shirts and the like, all with Reggae themes.

Nettle Bay Shopping Arcade.

La Casa del Habano. A shop that sells fine cigars, most imported from Cuba, but also from the Dominican Republic and Jamaica.

Marina.

Gingerbread Gallery. An art gallery that specializes in Haitian art. Original paintings and prints. Tapestries.

Marina.

Match. A supermarket selling pâtés, cheeses and other foods imported from France. Great for picnics.

Howell Center.

Le Goût du Vin (rue de Anguilla, near the Post Office). Sells imported French wine and champagne.

Beauty & Scents. Fragrances, cosmetics, and skincare products. Also includes a beauty salon.

Rue Général de Gaulle.

Banana Market Place. A small plaza near the library that sells locally made jewelry using black pearls, handmade clothing, rums and spices.

Marina L'Epicerie. A French delicatessen that sells caviar, smoked salmon, pâtés and Kedieard Petrossian products.

Maho Village

There is a small shopping center here. Shops stay open until 11 pm and are often open Sundays. Some are branch outlets of stores on Front Street.

There are inexpensive jewelry shops, a **Guavaberry** gift shop, **Lord and Hunter's** largest outlet that sells T-shirts, mugs, island spices and liquors, newspapers and household gifts. There's a **Starbucks** and **Häagen-Dazs** as well.

Art Galleries

French Side

Roland Richardson has galleries in Marigot (République) and Orleans; ☎ 590-87-84-08. The painter and native son has become a chronicler of the island's sights, traditions and people.

Minquet Gallery, Rambaud Hill (between Marigot and Grand Case), ☎ 590-87-76-06. Born in France but a long-time island resident, Minquet has won awards for paintings of the island's flora and its sights.

Dona Bryhiel Gallery is at Les Alizes, Oyster Pond, ☎ 590-87-43-93. Born in Marseille, the artist has had exhibits worldwide featuring her richly colored paintings of island life.

Other galleries include: **Graffitti**, with galleries in Marigot (Liberte) and on Blvd. Grand Case; **Galerie 105** and **Lynn Studio** are neighbors on Blvd. Grand Case. **Les Exotiques** in Oyster Pond exhibits and sells ceramics designed by Marie Moine, ☎ 590-29-53-76.

Dutch Side

Greenwith Gallery on Front Street, ☎ 599-542-3842, sells watercolors and lithographs depicting the island in "primitive" style.

Simpson Bay Art Gallery, Airport Road, ☎ 599-544-3464, has a large selection of paintings, lithographs and prints by local artists.

Best Places to Stay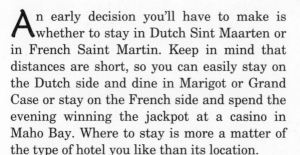

An early decision you'll have to make is whether to stay in Dutch Sint Maarten or in French Saint Martin. Keep in mind that distances are short, so you can easily stay on the Dutch side and dine in Marigot or Grand Case or stay on the French side and spend the evening winning the jackpot at a casino in Maho Bay. Where to stay is more a matter of the type of hotel you like than its location.

Generally, hotels on the Dutch side are high-rise resorts or large villa communities that can accommodate hundreds of guests (Maho Bay Beach Hotel has 600 guest rooms). They would be at home in Miami Beach, although they are individually located and not on one strip. The décor is contemporary, without traditional Caribbean architecture or furnishings. Instead you will find satellite TVs, in-room safes, stocked mini-bars, several restaurants, shops and on-property casinos. There are a few guest houses and inns and a growing number of developments that involve time-sharing options. While there is no hard sell, you will be reminded of this by the sales desks.

Established French-side hotels are in low-rise buildings – often two-story attached buildings set in landscaped grounds. Painted in pastel colors with peaked roofs and traditional gingerbread trim, they have wicker and rattan furnishings and private patios or terraces. They normally have kitchenettes. Even the cluster of moderately priced hotels recently built on Nettlé Bay are in this traditional style, although they are larger and some accommodate over 100 guests, a rarity on the French side. There are villa communities here, many of them near Orient Bay, but no time-shares.

Hotels on both sides of the island have English-speaking staff.

🔲 TIP

You should inquire about special air/hotel packages and be aware that rates in high season are as much as 30% more than off-season. Also note that a few hotels on the French side close for a time in the summer to allow for refurbishing and for staff vacations.

Villa Rentals

There are many more hotel rooms available on St. Martin, so villa rentals are not as popular as they are on St. Barts, where rooms are limited. However, there are individually owned villas and condos that can be rented by those who prefer the seclusion these accommodations offer.

Rental Agencies

Carimo, rue Charles de Gaulle, Marigot, ☎ 590-87-57-58; fax 590-51-02-45.

MountainWaves, ☎ 888-349-7800, www.mountainwaves.com.

Jennifer Vacation Villas, Simpson Bay Yacht Club, ☎ 599-544-3107; fax 599-544-3375.

Pierres Caraïbes, rue Kennedy, Marigot, ☎ 590-51-02-85.

Re/Max has several offices on the island. In Simpson Bay, ☎ 599-544-4580; in Oyster Pond, ☎ 599-543-6160; in Marigot, ☎ 590-87-00-04.

Sint Maarten/St. Martin

▣ TIP

Hotels on the Dutch side add a 5% tax to all hotel bills and a 10% to 15% service charge as well. French-side hotels add a *taxe de séjour* (visitor's tax) to hotel bills. Although it varies from hotel to hotel, it is often 5% per person. They also add a 10% to 15% service charge.

Hotels accept major credit cards, although a few small spots require a cash (check) deposit when making reservations.

Alive Price Scale

The scale below is based on prices for a double room in high season without taxes or surcharges. It is designed to give you a heads-up about hotel rates so you can select a spot within your budget, but you should always call to check current prices.

Deluxe . . . . Over $400

Expensive . . . . $250-$400

Moderate . . . . $150-$249

Inexpensive . . . . under $150

Seasonal Concerns

High season is November 15 through April 15. Off-season rates are as much as 30% less, and there are special packages available year-round.

The Best Hotels on Saint Martin

La Samanna
B.P. 4077, Baie Lounge
St. Martin, FWI 97064
☎ 590-87-64-00; fax 590-87-87-86
Deluxe

The islands of the Caribbean house many world-class resorts – none more elegant, understated and thoughtfully run than La Samanna. Consider these amenities: a staff member meets you at the airport, a cool welcoming drink awaits you in the lobby, fresh fruits and flowers appear in your room each day, and there is a guest library and video collection for use in your room.

Set on 55 acres of pristine beachfront on Baie Longue (Long Bay), one of St. Martin's loveliest beaches, this 81-room hideaway was inspired by the architecture of the Greek Islands. Your first glimpse of La Samanna's whitewashed buildings with their columns and archways will indeed remind you of Greece.

Management of the resort has been in the hands of the Orient Express Hotels Group since 1996. There are 16 Mediterranean-style villas that house one- , two- and three-bedroom suites. Surrounded by beautiful landscaping and gardens, the whitewashed villas have private terraces and patios. Interior curved archways and high ceilings allow the sunlight to brighten each room. Whatever your selection, you'll find comfortable wicker and rattan furnishings, colorful island art and accessories. The bathrooms are huge, with showers for two and dressing areas. The kitchenette is furnished and the refrigerator fully stocked.

For the first time since the resort opened over 30 years ago, new accommodations have been added and even more are on the drawing board. Four new suites and four-bedroom villas with private pools have been added. Furnishings were imported from the Philippines. Great care has been taken to make sure these new accommodations do not change the resort's ambience.

Closed Sept. & Oct.

La Samanna restaurant, a fine French spot (see *Dining*, page 230), is on a covered terrace overlooking the beach and pool. Most guests opt for the beach view, where umbrella-covered beach chairs stand. The watersports center has gear for guests' use and arranges fishing and scuba trips. A picnic lunch can be brought to your terrace or beach chair.

Three tennis courts can be lit for night play and there is a pro. Guests head to the fitness center, which is open from 7 am to 7 pm daily.

The extremely popular **Elysée Spa** offers beauty treatments as well as massages, facials and wraps (see *Sunup to Sundown*, page 171).

回 NOTE

With the hotel being expanded along the beach, construction is likely to continue for some time. The bulk of the work is done when the hotel is closed in September and October, however, so the noise will never affect your stay.

Over the years many international celebrities have been guests at La Samanna. They come not to "be seen," but for the privacy offered them. You'll appreciate the same.

★ TIP

La Samanna does offer special packages, so inquire about them. Be aware that there are minimum stay requirements at Christmas, New Year's and Easter.

Le Méridien
BP 581, Anse Marcel
St. Martin, FWI 97056
☎ 590-87-67-00; fax 590-87-30-38;
www.west-indies-online.com/Meridien/rooms.html
Expensive
On the island's northeastern shore, Marcel Cove, with a wide half-mile-long beach, is home

to several hotels. The largest is Le Meridien, which is like a small village. The entrance to the cove is down a steep hill that has a guarded entrance. From atop the hill, you'll see lots of red and yellow peaked rooftops and a busy marina. These are the two- and three-story buildings that house almost 400 rooms.

The original buildings in L'Habitation are in typical Creole style with gingerbread trim and open terraces; they contain 250 rooms. They are small but attractively furnished with colorful fabrics, area rugs and marble baths. The newer buildings, in Le Domaine, are more contemporary in design but have antique reproduction furniture, lots of island ceramics and curtained baths. The Marina Suites have full kitchens. All the rooms are air-conditioned and have fans, mini-bars and refrigerators.

All have private patios or terraces, but surprisingly few of them have ocean views.

Each area has a large swimming pool, Jacuzzi and sundeck, but it is the beach strip that is exceptional. The bay is busy with snorkelers, paddleboats, canoes, sunfloats, Jet Skis and windsurfers. The waterfront staff is very helpful. Other facilities include six tennis courts, four squash courts, two racquetball courts, an archery target and a gym. Guests here get special rates at the Privilège Spa nearby.

The main building, centrally located, looks like a plantation house. It is quite large, all marble and has marble staircases leading to the mezzanine level. The lobby has comfortable sofas and chairs, shops and a concierge.

The resort has four restaurants plus several bars. **La Belle France** is the upscale French restaurant. **La Veranda** serves Italian food and **Le Barbecue** serves salads, sandwiches and the like. Head to **Le Balaou** for a buffet breakfast. Local bands often play at night and at special theme dinners.

> ### 🔲 TIP
> Le Méridien is popular with French guests, and you'll find fewer English-speaking people here than at other places.

Le Privilège Resort and Spa
Anse Marcel
St. Martin, FWI 97150
☎ 590-87-38-38; fax 590-87-44-12;
www.privilege-spa.com
Expensive

Sharing Marcel Cove with Le Méridien, Le Privilège Resort and Spa sits on the hillside overlooking the larger hotel and the bay. The hotel has seemingly fallen on hard times and has sold off one section of the resort that stands on an adjoining hillside. That 20-room hotel, named the Marquis Resort and Spa, is under separate management. The Privilège now has 20 deluxe rooms and suites in two-story pink stucco buildings that have typical gingerbread trim. The rooms are large and elegantly furnished with rattans, island woods and floral accessories. Some have king-sized beds, marble bathrooms, in-room safes and CD players.

Rooms on the lower levels have patios, while the suites have terraces with ocean views.

Most guests here opt for the Spa Packages, which include accommodation, transfers, breakfast, dinner and various spa treatments. There are packages available for three, four, five and seven nights. The hotel also has a fully equipped gym, pool, tennis courts and exercise classes.

The Health Spa offers massages (including shiatsu), anti-cellulite treatments, seaweed body masks and beauty treatments.

Hotel Privilège (Marina)
Marina Anse Marcel
St. Martin, FWI 97150
☎ 590-87-37-37; fax 590-87-33-75;
www.west-indies-online.com/Privilege-Marina/default.html
Inexpensive

Yes, there are two hotels with the same name on Anse Marcel. This, the four-star one, shares the bay area with the deluxe Le Méridien, while its neighbor is on the hillside above the bay. This small (16-suite) hotel was built in Creole-style as six cottages, all with gingerbread trim on the rooftops and wide terraces. Suites include duplexes, doubles and juniors and all share contemporary furniture with light woods, fabrics and floors. Rooms are very clean and bright, with views of the marina and bay. All have kitchenettes and guests can use the beach and beach chairs at Anse Marcel without charge. There is no pool. The concierge here arranges all watersports, including motorboat rentals and day charters.

L'Esplanade Caraïbes Hotel
Grand Case
St. Martin, FWI 97150
☎ 590-87-06-55; fax 590-87-29-15
Moderate/Expensive

A personal favorite, L'Esplanade is small and its architecture is not the typical Creole design. The eye-catching structure sits on a hillside not far from the town of Grand Case. It is beautifully maintained and spotless. The staff is always dusting, polishing and especially gardening. A magnificent rock garden filled with colorful tropical flowers surrounds the sundeck and pool area.

The hotel has 24 rooms in parallel two-story Mediterranean-style buildings. The central courtyard serves as the reception area. Accommodations include studios and suites, some with loft bedrooms and some duplexes. They have king-sized beds, cathedral ceilings and mahogany staircases to the sleeping or office alcoves. There are sleeper sofas in the living rooms. Furnishings are contemporary and terraces front each suite. Each has a satellite TV, in-room safe and modern bath.

Stone staircases lead from the lobby level to the pool and sundeck. No beach or restaurant, but the beach and scores of restaurants are just minutes away, even on foot.

Grand Case Beach Club
Grand Case
St. Martin, FWI 97150
☎ 590-87-51-87; fax 590-87-59-93;
www.grandcasebeachclub.com
Moderate

With its lovely location on a secluded cove adjacent to Grand Case Village and its friendly American management, the Beach Club offers 72 studios and 15 one- or two-bedroom suites in a series of teal and white low-rise buildings. Three of the buildings are on Grand Case Beach and another is on the Club's second beach, Petit Plage, where a new restaurant, boutique and watersports center are now located. Suites have kitchens and some studios have sleeping lofts. All rooms have air-conditioning, satellite TVs and private terraces fronted by sliding glass doors. There is a pool and tennis court. Continental breakfast can be served in your room. The restaurant serves pasta and burgers. Ask for an ocean view. The mysterious shape on the horizon is Anguilla.

Closed Sept.

Anchorage Little Key Hotel
Cul de Sac
St. Martin, FWI 97150
☎ 590-29-55-55; fax 590-87-49-23
Expensive

On a secluded bay, Little Key Beach Hotel was completed in 1997. This is a deluxe resort with a very modern main building. There are only 94 spacious units; each is air-conditioned and has a refrigerator and large terrace. Furnishings are Creole-style with wicker, rattan and florals predominating. There are three pools, a terrace restaurant and bar, a health club and gym, and an activity program. A watersports center sits on the beach at the base of the hillside. Ferries from this beach go to uninhabited Lilet Pinel, where there is excellent snorkeling.

Mississippi
Oyster Pond
Saint Martin, FWI 97150
☎ 590-87-33-81; fax 590-87-31-52;
www.lemississippi.com
Moderate-Expensive
Unlike your typical Creole hotel, Mississippi is not painted in pastels but uses glossy woods on its terraces and walls and in its lobby. It really stands out.

The hotel is very small, with only 13 one- or two-bedroom suites in attached two-level buildings topped by green peaked roofs with gingerbread trim and carved terraces. The suites are large and have king-sized beds, rattan sofas and chairs with floral pillows and drapes, TVs, VCRs and stereo systems. There is a stocked mini-bar, a refrigerator and microwave and air-conditioning. The bathrooms, of pink Portuguese marble, have oversized bathtubs with Jacuzzis. Each suite has a terrace that faces the pool and sea.

Sint Maarten/St. Martin

The lobby is small but attractive, with a gleaming wood reception desk, wicker furniture and track lights. The pool is just a few steps away and is long enough for lap swimming. Lounge chairs of dark wood are covered by dark blue pads; the same wood is used on the beach umbrellas and adjacent bar and restaurant. **Le Mahogany restaurant** is quite elegant at night; it serves grilled meats, salads and Creole dishes.

The hotel is near the marina but a long walk away from a beach. Taking a car is the best option.

Hotel Beach Plaza
Baie de Marigot
Saint Martin, FWI 97150
☎ 590-87-87-00; fax 590-87-18-87
Moderate

The Beach Plaza is not an elegant stop, but it does have a lot to offer. It is on Sandy Ground Road, just a five-minute walk to Marigot, with a small sandy beach on Marigot Bay where you can tan, swim or enjoy a pedal boat. The hotel's major asset is its long freshwater pool and sundeck.

All the hotel's public rooms are off the pink tiled lobby, which is glass-topped and has plants and ponds that lend a greenhouse effect. The piano bar and restaurant are here, along with shops and car rental agencies.

The 154 rooms (including some suites and deluxe studios) are on the three upper floors. Open terraces allow the rooms to be visible from the lobby level. Rooms have floral bedspreads and drapes, light wood furniture, air-conditioners, refrigerators and small satellite TVs.

Terraces front every room, facing either the sea or the marina.

Captain Oliver's Resort
Oyster Pond
Saint Martin, FWI 97150
☎ 590-87-40-26; fax 590-87-40-84;
www.captainolivers.com
Moderate-Expensive

Captain Oliver's Resort is one of the island's most popular hideaways, and deservedly so. Its terrific location, attractive rooms, excellent restaurant and active marina are all pluses, but it's an intangible – perhaps its Gallic charm – that makes it so alluring. There is a Captain Oliver, and his resort has straddled the French-Dutch border for almost 20 years. The hotel's 50 junior suites are in the French West Indies, while the restaurant is built on a jetty over the horseshoe-shaped bay, which is in Dutch waters.

In an attempt to make the resort look like a ship, wood plank bridges with rope handrails lead from the comfortable lobby to the hotel area and to the restaurant. The suites, with ocean or marina views, are large, light and airy. White is the predominant color on the walls, tile floors, bamboo furniture and peaked beamed ceilings. Colorful floral bedcovers and drapes add an island touch. Each suite is air-conditioned and has a private terrace where you can enjoy breakfast, included in the rate. Suites have king-sized or twin beds, mini-bar, kitchenette and satellite TV.

Captain Oliver's restaurant (see *Dining*, page 250) specializes in Creole dishes, particularly seafood. The hotel offers shuttle service to nearby beaches. The marina (see *Sunup to Sundown*, page 276) has shops, including a grocery.

Alizea
Mont Vernon
St. Martin, FWI 97150
☎ 590-87-33-42; fax 590-87-41-15;
www.alizeahotel.com
Moderate

The name Alizea was taken from Les Alizes, the trade winds that cool these islands and blow gently across the terraces of this hilltop hotel. Surrounded by lush tropical plants and flowers, Alixea has a stunning view of Orient Bay, but it's removed from the beach's frenetic pace. Because it is small, guests get to know one another and the friendly owners make everyone feel right at home.

Each of the 18 studios and the eight one-bedroom bungalows are tastefully decorated with small touches that give each its own style. You'll find wickers, carved headboards, wood-beamed ceilings with fans and colorful wall hangings. Every room has a kitchenette and an oversized terrace. The **Alizea restaurant** is one of the island's best. It serves French, Creole and Vietnamese food. The Alizea has a pool and there is a path to the beach. It's a 15-minute walk.

La Plantation
Orient Bay
Saint Martin, FWI 97150
☎ 590-29-58-00; fax 590-29-58-08;
www.la-plantation.com
Moderate-Expensive
La Plantation's location, set back just a few feet from the bustling restaurants and watersports centers of Orient Beach, may not be your cup of tea if you're looking for peace and quiet. The action starts early and goes on well into the night. The inn, surrounded by banana trees, consists of a series of one-story Colonial-style villas; each has two studios and one suite. It looks like a Creole motel with pastel walls and white verandas, but the suites are surprisingly attractive. Decorated in pastel-colored rattan furniture with comfortable cushions you can really sink into, each is air-conditioned, has a modern kitchen and bath, satellite TV and in-room safe. The inn has a swimming pool, although most guests head to the nearby beach. Continental breakfast is included.

Mont Vernon Hotel
Box 1174 Orient Bay
St. Martin, FWI 97062
☎ 590-87-62-00; fax 590-87-37-27
Moderate-Expensive
On an exposed bluff high above Orient Bay, the hotel sprawls across the hilltop, with its main

pastel building at the core and a score of tri-level attached buildings around it. Named for Caribbean islands, those that face the ocean – Guadeloupe, Aruba and Antigua – have great views. Mont Vernon is an all-suite hotel that has 338 junior suites and 32 Atlantic suites. These are larger and have two bedrooms. All the suites are good sized, have rattan and wicker furniture, refrigerator and TV. All are air-conditioned and have a private terrace covered by a gingerbread rooftop.

A beehive of activity, the hotel has a large swimming pool and sundeck, tennis courts, Ping-Pong tables, dartboards and a fitness center. It's a short stroll to the beach where sand volleyball games draw lots of players and lots of kibitzers and where the watersports center has all kinds of gear to rent.

The lobby is large but often filled with tour groups. Lunch is served at The Sloop at poolside, while a buffet breakfast and dinner are served at La Créole in the main building.

Hotel Anchorage Margot
Baie Nettlé
St. Martin, FWI 97150
☎ 590-87-92-01; fax 590-87-92-13
Moderate
Although it has 96 rooms, the Anchorage Margot has managed to retain a smaller, more intimate French ambience. The grounds, with lots of palm trees and flowering plants, are

immaculate. The eight three-story Creole buildings are connected by brick walkways. It is their design that sets them apart. They zig-zag to create more room and each terrace or patio (every unit has one) has some privacy and an unobstructed garden or beach view. You'll find browns and corals on the sofas, barrel chairs and bedspreads and French shutter doors to the terrace. All are air-conditioned, have TV (no satellite), VCR, safe and refrigerator.

There are two swimming pools with Jacuzzis and the attractive **Entre Deux Mers** restaurant is set between them. American breakfasts, drinks and dinner are served here.

Quieter than its neighbors, Anchorage Margot is a good choice.

> ### 🔲 TIP
> The hotel has a small beach on Simpson Lagoon where you can Jet Ski or windsurf.

Le Flamboyant
Nettlé Bay
St. Martin, FWI 97150
☎ 590-87-60-00; fax 590-87-99-57;
www.leflamboyant.com
Moderate

Le Flamboyant's occupancy rate is high year-round because it offers good value. Though not luxurious, its 271 suites are scattered in a score of two-story red-roofed buildings, leaving a lot of open space filled by stone pathways and attractive landscaping. The comfortable lobby is adjacent to the large pool, sundeck and beachfront restaurant, **La Terrasse**, which serves lunch and dinner as well as buffets on theme nights.

An all-suite hotel, the junior suites can sleep three, while the larger one- and two-bedroom suites can sleep four to six people. All are air-conditioned and some have kitchenettes, often popular with families that have young children. Every suite has a balcony. Those facing the lagoon are slightly more expensive.

There are two pools (one for children), tennis courts, and a fitness center. Organized activities include water aerobics, water and basket polo and beach volleyball. There is a children's playground.

Le Flamboyant has a 1,200-foot stretch of beach on Simpson Lagoon (across the water is Dutch Sint Maarten) where you can windsurf, paddle a kayak or just swim.

回 TIP

If you like your water with waves, there's a shuttle service to nearby Baie Rouge, a stunning beach.

Mercure Simson Beach
BP 172 Nettlé Bay
St. Martin, FWI 97150
☎ 590-87-54-54; fax 590-87-92-11;
www.mercure-simpson-beach.com
Moderate

Another of the hotels along the Baie Nettlé
strip, the Mercure draws many European
guests who like the moderate price and the
family oriented atmosphere. The large lobby,
with blue wicker sofas and chairs and bright
yellow floral pillows, is often crowded with
guests and children. Accommodations are in
three-story attached buildings surrounded by
tropical plants and trees. There are 120 studios
that can sleep two adults and one child and 45
one-bedroom suites that can accommodate two
adults and two children. Each one is air-
conditioned, has a kitchenette, and has a terrace facing the beach or the garden. The
ground-floor rooms have patios.

Days here begin with a large buffet breakfast
served at the poolside **LaViBo Kaye Restaurant**. There is also a children's pool. Families
wile away the day at the beach on the lagoon.
The watersports center has pedal boats, sea
scooters, Jet Skis and snorkel gear. There are
tennis courts, Ping-Pong tables, volleyball
courts and *pétanque* (the French equivalent of
bocce). The staff organizes activities for adults
and children. The restaurant often has theme
nights.

Blue Beach Hotel

26 Oyster Pond
St. Martin, FWI 97150
☎ 590-87-33-44; fax 590-87-42-13
Moderate

Nestled on the hillside near Oyster Pond Bay overlooking the Atlantic and the Oyster Pond Marina, the 19 rooms and suites in the red-roofed Creole-style bungalows are comfortable but without any frills. Air-conditioned, each has a kitchenette and private terrace. There is a large pool and sundeck, and a poolside restaurant called Frogs that serves French and Creole food. Many guests at Blue Beach are scuba divers, sailors or fishermen involved in programs at the marina.

Pavillon Beach Hotel

BP 313 Grand Case
St. Martin, FWI 97150
☎ 590-87-96-46; fax 590-87-71-04;
www.pavillonbeach.com
Moderate

At the heart of Grand Case, the Pavillon has six studios, 10 one-bedroom suites and one deluxe honeymoon suite with a king-sized bed. Decorated in warm pastels and rattan, each unit has a kitchenette, air-conditioning, an in-room safe, a TV (no satellite) and a modern bathroom, shower only. Continental breakfast is served in your room.

But best of all, every room has a terrace or patio that faces the sea. Ground-floor patios open right onto the sand. A nondescript choice with a good location.

Sint Maarten/St. Martin

Hevea

163 Blvd. Grand Case
St. Martin, FWI 97150
☎ 590-87-56-85; fax 590-87-83-88
Moderate

The Hevea name is most associated with the gourmet French restaurant that occupies the front rooms of this restored Creole mansion. The eight-room inn, owned by the same family, is marked by the awning-covered walkway. The rooms are tiny like so many on Paris' Left Bank, but each is distinctive. They have wood-beamed ceilings and carved mahogany headboards and dressers. There are colorful wall-hangings and ceramic pieces in each room. Bathrooms are modern and a small patio or terrace fronts each room. The three suites have kitchenettes and there are also three studios and two double rooms. Only five are air-conditioned; the others have ceiling fans. Breakfast, included in the rate, is served in the charming Creole sitting room. The inn is across the street from Grand Case Beach and scores of restaurants are within strolling distance.

Guests get discounts on dinner at Hevea (see page 247).

Hotel Atlantide

Box 5140 Grand Case
St. Martin, FWI 97150
☎ 590-87-09-80; fax 590-87-12-36
Moderate

Fronting Grand Case Boulevard, the Atlantide looks out of place. It is a modern building with none of the French-Creole architecture that makes other stops here so attractive. So it was a pleasant surprise to find 10 bright and airy studios and suites with terraces that look out on Grand Case Beach. Studios have a double bed and a small sitting area. Suites have one or two bedrooms. They have light pastel walls and floral or striped furnishings. Kitchenettes have dining bars. You can also eat on the terrace, which has folding wood doors to keep out the light. The hotel has lounge chairs and umbrellas on the beach.

Morning Star Guest House
Grand Case
Saint Martin, FWI 97150
☎ 590-87-93-85; fax 590-87-72-08
Inexpensive
A family-run guest house on the main road just before the town, Morning Star has nine rooms. Each is air-conditioned and has a fully equipped kitchenette and daily maid service. No frills, but friendly owners and staff. You can walk to the beach and the restaurants in town in five minutes.

A Clothing-Optional Resort

Club Orient Naturist Resort
Orient Bay
St. Martin, FWI 97150
☎ 590-87-33-85; fax 590-87-33-76
Expensive-Moderate

In the film *A Shot in the Dark,* Inspector Clouseau pursues a murder suspect into a resort, unaware that it is strictly a nudist camp. Hilarity follows. Club Orient is clothing-optional, but we opted to keep ours on while looking through. The 47 waterfront beach chalets had formerly been built in red pine imported from Finland, but were rebuilt after Hurricane Luis in concrete. They are safer, but not as attractive, although they have retained the size and design. The studios and suites have been rebuilt in pine because they are not as exposed to the elements. Also rebuilt is the **Papagayo Restaurant**, which looks even more attractive. Once again there is a watersports center, grocery and boutique. The club offers lots of activities for both daytime and evening.

There are two other choices in Marigot. **Le Royale Louisiana** on rue Charles de Gaulle (☎ 590-87-86-51) and **La Résidence**, also on rue Charles de Gaulle (☎ 590-87-70-37). Rather basic, they are built around inner courtyards that have restaurants.

Inexpensive.

Villa Communities

Green Cay Village

Box 3006 Orient Bay
St. Martin, FWI 97064
☎ 590-87-38-63; fax 590-87-39-27;
www.greencayvillage.com
Expensive

The most upscale of the villa communities at Orient Bay, Green Cay Village is set back from the beach itself on a nearby hillside. There are 16 clustered villas that hold 48 accommodations with one to three bedrooms. Each cluster has its own pool and sundeck with lounge chairs. The three-bedroom villas have two bedrooms with king-sized beds and a third with a double bed.

Painted in soft pastels with a gingerbread trim, they are quite modern inside with tile floors small area rugs, cable TVs and comfortable wicker furniture. Kitchens are fully equipped with all major appliances as well as a blender, a microwave, a barbecue grill and a coffeemaker. A first night "starter kit" of food is a nice touch. Views from the living room terrace include the beach and St. Barts.

> ### 🔲 TIP
>
> Green Cay guests have special rates at the rental shops and restaurants on Orient Bay, and can charge items to their room.

Nettlé Bay Beach Club
BP 4081, Nettlé Bay
St. Martin, FWI 97064
☎ 590-87-68-89; fax 590-87-21-51
Moderate-Expensive

Centrally located between Marigot and Maho Bay, Nettlé Bay Beach Club is a good choice if you like the privacy of villa living but want hotel amenities. Attractive with gray wood exteriors and white shutters and trim on the peaked rooftops, the attached beach villas are set in three large horseshoe-shaped clusters with the open end facing the sea. Each cluster has its own pool and sundeck complete with lounge chairs. Others are on the beach just a few steps away. The ground level of each villa has one or two bedrooms and a kitchenette. The walls are painted in pastels. There are tiled floors and contemporary rattan furnishings in the living room. Each veranda faces the pool and sea. On the second level, the villa studios have queen-sized beds and small sundecks. There are 200 villa accommodations.

The fourth cluster is a seven-building semi-circle called The Gardens. Each garden building has five units, smaller and less expensive than the villas. Lower level suites have king-sized beds and small sitting areas. Upper level rooms have queen-sized beds. Both have kitchenettes. An attractive garden area and pool are in the central courtyard.

There are three tennis courts on property and a watersports center nearby that offers Nettlé Bay guests special rates.

Le Grand Bleu, the beachside restaurant, shares the local dining scene with **La Parilla**, which serves Argentine-style grilled meats, and the French and Creole **La Fayette**.

Esmeralda Resort
Box 5141, Orient Bay
St. Martin, FWI 97071
☎ 590-87-36-36; fax 590-87-35-18;
www.esmeralda-resort.com
Moderate-Expensive

Although it looks like a suburban housing development, Esmeralda is actually an attractive villa community that operates as a hotel. Fifteen villas, comprised of 54 rooms and suites, offer all the comforts of a home and the amenities of a resort. Each of the villa clusters has its own swimming pool and Jacuzzi. Functionally decorated with rust tile floors, pale yellow walls and colorful florals on the sofas, chairs and coverlets, the villas are designed for families. The suites, with two to five bedrooms, have fully equipped kitchens and king, queen and twin beds. Rooms and suites can be joined to form larger units. There is daily maid service, satellite TV and a concierge to offer sightseeing trips and arrange for babysitting if necessary. Esmeralda has a small beach with a watersports center and it is just a short walk to Orient Beach and its restaurants. There are two lighted tennis courts and a good on-property restaurant, **L'Astrolobe**. You can enjoy breakfast and dinner (French) here.

The Best Hotels on Sint Maarten

Oyster Bay Beach Resort
Box 239
Sint Maarten, Netherlands Antilles
☎ 599-543-6084; fax 599-543-6695;
www.oysterbaybeachresort.com
Expensive

Heading east from Princess Juliana Airport and Philipsburg, you'll pass the Old Salt Pond that made Sint Maarten so important to the Dutch and West Indies communities with great names such as Sucker Garden and Naked Boy Hill. Soon you'll see the turn-off for Dawn Beach and Oyster Pond. Narrow and potholed, it's not what you'd expect. But, at the top of yet another rise, a mirage appears. It's on the Dutch side of Oyster Pond but looks like something from French Morocco. A whitewashed building with Moorish arches and two stone towers is set on a promontory surrounded by green hills and calm blue waters. The lobby, with sturdy white wicker sofas, rocking chairs and tables, is between the towers and an open courtyard is just beyond it. The courtyard has a bar and umbrella-covered tables and the candlelit gourmet French restaurant.

The original 20 rooms (built when the hotel was the Oyster Pond Beach Hotel) are in the main building. Six are on the ground level and the others on the second floor around a white walkway with dark wooden balustrades. Named for famous old sailing ships, they have patios or terraces; a few are duplex. The newer Ocean Suites sit along the narrowing bluff. They are larger and more luxuriously appointed, but the façades are not Moorish. Each air-conditioned guest room has white wicker furniture, rust tile floors, French pastel fabrics and colorful lithographs. Hairdryers, small refrigerators and bathrobes are also standard. Suites have tubs, while studios have only showers.

The scene has changed dramatically here since the last edition. Some 130 new rooms have been added, and the resort now looks like a town. It's so different from our last visit that we assumed we had missed the Oyster Pond turn-off. The original 40-room structure is still here and is the heart of the complex. The new rooms are in condo-style buildings across the road and along the beach. Many of those one- and two-bedroom suites have been sold to individual owners, while others are time-shares and rentals. They are modern in décor and full of amenities, but without the pizzazz of the original rooms. Not our cup of tea, this new resort still has a magnificent location between Oyster Pond and Dawn Beach, a new larger swimming pool and a fine Cantonese restaurant. Try for a room in the 40-room building. It's the reason we haven't moved this one to the "Time Share Resorts" section.

Maho Beach Hotel & Casino
Maho Bay
Sint Maarten, Netherlands Antilles
☎ 599-555-2115; fax 599-545-3180
Expensive

If you're going on vacation but don't want to get away from it all, the Maho Beach Hotel Complex is for you. It's not just a hotel, it's a village. The hotel itself has 600 guest rooms, 400 of which are in a newer wing. These are housed in a cluster of pink and white high-rise buildings with views of the sea, landscaped gardens and the village. Rooms are large, have cable TV and contemporary furnishings without a hint of Creole style. Some have king-sized beds. All rooms have private terraces.

> ### 💥 WARNING
> One important drawback here is the runway of Princess Juliana Airport, which is adjacent to the grounds. If you like to sleep in, ask for a room in the west wing.

The facilities at Maho have to be larger than life to accommodate guests. There are three pools, lots of lounge chairs both on the beach and on pool sundecks, three tennis courts, a hot tub and a well-stocked and well-staffed waterfront center. There are lots of organized activities as well. To cool off, you can have a drink at the swim-up bar.

The complex has 10 restaurants, including cafés, pizzerias, and gourmet continental and Italian spots. The shopping center has three sections and includes jewelers, a deli, local handicrafts and resortwear/T-shirt shops.

Adjacent to the large, comfortable hotel lobby, is the Royal Islander Club, with its own 130 timeshare apartments and pool.

After dinner you can visit the on-property theater, disco, or the largest casino on the island, the Casino Royale.

It's not for everyone, but Maho is a unique experience – Greenwich Village on the sea.

Great Bay Beach Hotel & Casino
Box 310, Philipsburg
Sint Maarten, Netherlands Antilles
☎ 599-542-2446; fax 599-542-3008;
www.greatbayhotel.com
Expensive-Moderate
The Great Bay Beach Hotel & Casino is on a small peninsula at the western tip of Great Bay, just a 10-minute stroll from Philipsburg, and fronts the heart of the bay. It has 285 rooms, each with a private patio or terrace. Rooms are good size, air-conditioned, have satellite TVs and contemporary furnishings with not a Creole touch in sight. However, you'll see the Creole style in the very large, plant-filled lobby, which features wicker furniture with

pink pillows to match the striped awnings over the open-air arches facing Philipsburg. Many guests enjoy colorful tropical drinks here in the afternoon.

The hotel has two freshwater pools with sundecks and lounge chairs. Additional chairs are on the adjacent beach. The young staff has waterskis, windsurfers, WaveRunners and sailboats, and even gives pool scuba lessons in the pool. Organized activities include pool aerobics and beach volleyball, as well as a host of other games. There are Ping-Pong tables, shuffleboard and tennis courts, and a fitness center.

The hotel has several dining options as well as beach barbecues and theme night parties. After dinner, guests head to the nightclub or casino in the hotel or those in Philipsburg. Taxis are always available at the hotel and you can find parking in town at night.

Princess Port de Plaisance Resort & Casino

Union Road, Cole Bay
Sint Maarten, Netherlands Antilles
☎ 599-544-5222; fax 599-544-2284;
www.princessportdeplaisance.com
Expensive

This differs from the two hotels above, which are in centers of activity on Dutch Sint Maarten. Port de Plaisance, on a private island jutting into Simpson Bay, is off the beaten track, but within 10 minutes of Maho Bay and Philipsburg and 20 minutes from Marigot.

Many guests arrive at the resort and never leave the premises (except to shop), and it isn't hard to imagine why.

An all-suite resort, with 88 junior, one- and two-bedroom units, it has vast grounds. All rooms overlook the freeform pool and sundeck, with cascading waterfalls, pool bar and grill. Rooms are furnished with contemporary light woods and fabrics and all have fully equipped kitchenettes, cable TVs, in-room safes and oversized beds. Bathrooms are stocked with deluxe amenities. A full American breakfast buffet is included in your rate.

The hotel grounds are beautifully landscaped with tropical vegetation, rock formations and walkways. They house several restaurants, including a health bar and evening entertainment center. An independent Italian eaterie, **Dario's** is across a wooden footbridge from the hotel.

Daytime hours can be spent poolside or at the health and tennis club. There are seven courts (all can be lit for night play), as well as a pro. There is a fully equipped gym, lap pool, sauna, steam room and organized fitness classes. All of the above are free to guests.

There are individual charges for visits to the spa, which has a beauty salon and rooms for massages, facials and wraps. If you aren't pooped out by dusk, you can walk over another footbridge to Sint Maarten's largest casino. It has more games than any other on the island.

There is also a fully equipped marina on the property. "Port de Plaisance" means Pleasure Port and indeed this new resort offers lots of that.

Timeshare Resorts

Timesharing is ubiquitous on Dutch Sint Maarten. The option is offered in huge resort complexes, in the tiny 14-room Mary's Boon Inn and even at the luxurious Oyster Bay Resort. We have detailed only a few of the resorts that also operate as hotels.

Pelican Resort & Casino
Box 431 Simpson Bay
☎ 599-544-2503; fax 599-544-2133
It has only 342 guest rooms, half the number of nearby Maho Beach Hotel, but the Pelican Resort looks much larger because the buildings that house the junior, one- and two-bedroom suites are scattered throughout the property and not clustered. You can easily get lost within the complex. Suites have air-conditioned bedrooms, cable TV, fully equipped kitchens with all major appliances, and contemporary furnishings. The living room and dining areas are cooled by ceiling fans and by breezes that flow over the sea and in from the private terrace. Pelican has five pools, including one for kids, two long beach strips and an open-sea marina. The watersports center is well stocked with gear. There is a deli, a market, a medical office,

a shopping arcade and barbecue grills. The four tennis courts can be lit for night play. There is a fitness center and a beauty salon. Restaurants include a steak and seafood house, a bistro and a café. There is a large casino.

Little Bay Beach Resort

Box 961, Philipsburg

☎ 599-542-2333; fax 599-542-5410

A deluxe choice operated by Divi Resorts, which is well known in Aruba and Bonaire, Little Bay is set on the tip of the peninsula that juts out into Great Bay. Secluded and romantic, it was so badly damaged by Hurricane Luis that it was closed for 1½ years and virtually rebuilt from the ground up. The effort was well worth it.

Guest rooms are set in three-story attached villas with whitewashed facades, red peaked rooftops and graceful archways. They overlook the bay or gardens. Accommodations range from comfortable studios to three-bedroom apartments. All have Louis XV furniture, pale tiled floors, and private patios or balconies. There are freshwater pools, several tennis courts with a pro, and a long beach with a watersports center. There are several on-property dining choices and you are only a few minutes from options in Philipsburg.

Royal Palm Beach Club

Airport Road, Simpson Bay
Sint Maarten, Netherlands Antilles
☎ 599-544-3737; fax 599-544-5588

A deluxe choice, the 140-room Royal Palm offers only one type of accommodation – a two-bedroom/two-bathroom suite in a modern low-rise attached villa on Kimsha Beach near Simpson Bay. The spacious suites, decorated attractively with rattans, wickers and floral fabrics, can sleep six comfortably and all have terraces that face the ocean. In-room amenities include air-conditioning, cable TV and VCR, fully equipped kitchen with all major appliances and a microwave and blender. There is a large pool and sundeck adjacent to the beach. It has a swim-up bar and a beachfront restaurant. There are communal picnic areas with barbecue grills, a health club and a well-stocked waterfront center. The hotel complex has a shopping arcade with a grocery store. The big surprise is that the Royal Palm does not have a good restaurant, but there are many nearby.

Caravanserai Beach Resort

Beacon Hill Road #2
Sint Maarten, Netherlands Antilles
☎ 599-545-4000; fax 599-544-4001;
www.caravanseraibeachresort.com
Expensive-Moderate

Set on Burgeaux Bay, near the airport and Maho Beach Village, the Caravanserai is a red-roofed resort on a wide promontory. It has 188 guest rooms in suites, deluxe one-bedroom suites and bungalows that can sleep six. The standard suites have contemporary furniture, are air-conditioned, and have cable TVs and mini-bars. The deluxe one-bedroom suites and bungalows have Caribbean florals and pastels, rattan and mahogany and marble bathrooms. They have fully equipped kitchens. All guest rooms have terraces. In the complex you will find three swimming pools and whirlpools, two tennis courts, a white sand beach and a good restaurant. Like a small town, it also has a small convention center and health spa.

Small Hotels

Mary's Boon Beach Plantation
117 Simpson Bay Road
Sint Maarten, Netherlands Antilles
☎ 599-545-4235; fax 599-545-3403;
www.marysboon.com
Inexpensive

A legendary stop, this cozy inn has 14 large studios on the beach, south of Princess Juliana Airport and Maho Village. Each is sparsely furnished but has all the necessities, including a kitchenette, private bath and a beachfront patio. They do not have air-conditioning, TV or phone.

The restaurant draws visitors as well as locals. The French/Creole dishes rely on the freshest ingredients so the menu is set each day. There is only one seating, at 8 pm, and you need reservations. Check the menu at that time. The restaurant is also not air-conditioned. Both the inn and the restaurant accept major credit cards.

Passangrahan Royal Guest House

The oldest inn on the island.

15 Front Street, Box 151 Philipsburg
Sint Maarten, Netherlands Antilles
☎ 599-542-3588; fax 599-542-2885
Inexpensive

An island treasure, this 30-room Colonial inn is in the heart of Philipsburg and on the beach.

The bar is named Sidney Greenstreet and it would not be a surprise to see Bogie and Bacall at the bar or on the wicker peacock chairs on the tiled veranda. No TV or phones in your room. There is a restaurant in addition to the bar. Inexpensive and charming.

★ DID YOU KNOW?

The green and white building of Passangrahan was formerly the governor's home, and Queen Wilhelmina stayed here when she visited the island.

Holland House Beach Hotel

43 Front Street, Philipsburg
Sint Maarten, Netherlands Antilles
☎ 599-542-2572; fax 599-542-4673;
www.hhbh.com
Inexpensive

A perfect choice for business travelers, Holland House is right in the middle of the shopping street in Philipsburg, which is crowded and bustling from early morning to early evening

Sint Maarten/St. Martin

six days a week. The biggest surprise is that Holland House is actually on a beach – Great Bay Beach – and its sandy strip has palm trees and beach chairs. Drinks and food are served on the open-air terrace at beachside. The hotel's 54 rooms and all the public areas are well-cared-for and the service at the front desk and restaurant is first rate. Rooms are air conditioned, with cable TV and kitchenettes. Terraces overlook the bay or Front Street. Business travelers will appreciate the 24-hour Internet access from the lobby computers and the state-of-the-art conference center. The hotel restaurant serves all three meals, but excellent restaurants, night spots and casinos are just a stroll away.

★ NOTE

Horizon View Beach Hotel, at 49 Front Street, is similar to Holland House. The hotel has 30 rooms and the reception area is on the second floor above the shops. Rooms are equipped with air conditioners, cable TVs and kitchenettes. It too has a small sand strip on Great Bay and rooms face the Bay or Front Street. Inexpensive. ☎ 599-543-2121; fax 599-542-0705.

Horny Toad Guest House
Box 30289 Simpson Bay
Sint Maarten, Netherlands Antilles
☎ 599-542-4323; fax 599-542-3316;
www.thehornytoadguesthouse.com
Inexpensive

A former governor's home that has been converted into eight comfortable units, each with
full equipped kitchen and a terrace that faces
Simpson Bay. Rooms have recently been refurbished and while there are few frills, they certainly are comfortable. There is daily maid
service.

Best Places to Eat

Food, glorious food, sang Oliver and his
mates in the musical version of *Oliver
Twist*. Unfortunately, they didn't have
enough to eat, something that will not be
your problem on this island where tourist
literature boasts of over "400 tantalizing
restaurants." That number may include
McDonald's and greasy spoons, but there is no
question that the island has a surprisingly
large number of restaurants. They include
elegant French bistros, brasseries, and cafés,
Italian, continental, Vietnamese and
American-style restaurants and a good number
that serve typical Creole specialties. You can
enjoy lunch and dinner overlooking a beach or
on one, near a busy marina or a bustling

shopping street or on the terrace of an elegant resort in a secluded cove.

The island's gastronomic center is on the French side. Marigot, which was a fishing village not so long ago, has over 50 restaurants in its "downtown." There are informal ones near the marina and port, and more formal ones in restored Creole buildings nearby. The tiny hamlet of Grand Case is not far behind with 20 superb international restaurants on its one main street. Many of these are owned and staffed by French expats, trained in the kitchens of France's finest restaurants. A bonus is that their cooking represents regional specialties from all over France.

There are no Dutch restaurants on the island, but Sint Maarten has fine international restaurants in Philipsburg and Maho, and a great many moderately priced American-style eateries along Simpson Bay as well.

Restaurants are risky businesses. A place can be "in" one year and gone the next. We have tried to select restaurants that have had staying power – some have been popular for 20 years. You'll surely find some hot new spots during your stay and we hope you'll alert us to them so that we can include them in the next edition.

Prices

Prices might be higher than you would expect. Keep in mind that everything here is imported, much of it from Europe, and the added costs are passed down. On the plus side, the prices here will still be less than you'd pay for comparable food and ambience in New York or Paris.

Dining Savvy

◉ Make reservations for dinner, particularly in high season. Restaurants are small. In some cases reservations are required.

◉ Restaurants accept major credit cards, traveler's checks and US dollars. Prices are listed in euros on the French side and in euros and US $ on the Dutch side.

◉ Restaurants on the French side typically serve lunch from noon to 3 pm, then close and re-open for dinner from 6:30 until 10:30 pm. Dutch-side restaurants do not close after lunch but serve all day. Many of the island's finest restaurants serve dinner only.

◎ Unlike St. Barts, where virtually every restaurant closes for a period in the off-season, only a few French restaurants follow that trend.

◎ Casual chic attire is the norm at the upscale dining spots. Jeans are very popular. Shorts and T-shirts are acceptable in the moderately priced eateries. Many restaurants post their menus at the door.

Alive Price Scale

This scale is based on a three-course dinner for one person without alcoholic beverages.

Very Expensive . . . . Over $60

Expensive . . . . $40-$60

Moderate . . . . $30-$40

Inexpensive . . . . Under $30

▣ TIP

Restaurants typically add a 10% to 15% service charge to the bill. It is common to leave a small additional tip for good service.

Restaurants in or Near Marigot

Mario's Bistro
Pont de Sandy Ground
☎ 590-87-06-36
Nouvelle French
Expensive

Just five minutes from Marigot, Mario's overlooks the canal that connects the ocean waters of Nettlé Bay with the calm waters of Simpson Bay Lagoon. One friend who winters here and another who lives here both picked Mario's as the island's best restaurant. It isn't the most elegant or even the most attractive, but the food and service are exceptional. The dining room and bar are on a roof-covered terrace with blue walls and blue tiled floors. The wood tables are near the canal so you can see the marine traffic. The menu changes frequently to take advantage of the freshest ingredients available. Some specialties include a chunky fish or vegetable soup or salmon sushi with steamed asparagus. The bouillabaisse is enough for two, and among the pasta dishes the penne with cherry tomatoes stands out. The lamb chops and other meats are tender enough to cut with a fork and desserts include tarts and fresh fruits. Reservations are a must since the restaurant is small and service unhurried.

Look for Sandy Point Bridge.

La Samanna Restaurant
Baie Longue
☎ 590-87-64-00
Classical French
Very Expensive
Everything about La Samanna Resort is understated. "When you have it, there's no need to flaunt it," could be their motto. And so it is with their gourmet French restaurant that rivals any of the independent restaurants on the island. Its setting is special as well. The restaurant is on a split-level terrace in the main building that looks out over the long crescent beach. You'll dine by candlelight surrounded by the red, purple and orange aromatic flowers of the Caribbean. Reservations are a must, but come early for a pre-dinner drink and to explore the grounds. A unique, albeit expensive, hors d'oeuvre is the caviar served with blini and chilled vodka. There are three kinds of caviar to choose from. Seafood risotto or chunks of lobster with curry butter are good starters. Main courses include an unusual surf 'n turf with beef tenderloins and lobster medallions in port wine and delicious tournedos of swordfish and tuna with five-peppercorn sauce. If you like duck, it is served with raspberry sauce and fried plantains. Desserts include pastries, tarts and ice cream. Long pants are required. The restaurant has a wine cellar reputed to hold 20,000 bottles. Reservations are a must in high season.

La Vie en Rose
Blvd. de France
☎ 590-87-54-42
French restaurant and café
Very Expensive

One of the first French restaurants on the island, La Vie en Rose has maintained its high standards and remains a delightful choice for a romantic dinner. On the second floor of a century-old warehouse that overlooks the harbor, the dining room is quite formal with pale pink walls and matching tablecloths. Its rattan chairs have floral cushions and antique wall sconces provide indirect lighting. Red-striped awnings shade the windows on every side of the dining room and the half-dozen tables on the outer terrace which are considered choice.

Start with the smoked salmon with porcini mushrooms, salmon roe and tomatoes or the chunky lobster salad with ginger. Move on to crayfish in puff pastry, the filet of swordfish with passion fruit sauce, or a mignon of lamb in venison sauce. Save room for apple tart or chocolate mousse cake.

La Vie en Rose Café is on the first floor and has an outdoor terrace on Market Square. Here they serve sandwiches, salads and delicious pastries well into the night. The patio tables, covered by umbrellas, are especially nice.

Sint Maarten/St. Martin

Jean Dupont Bistro
Port Royale Marina
☎ 590-87-71-13
French/Vietnamese
Lunch & dinner
Moderate

One of the more formal restaurants around the marina, Jean Dupont has both an inner dining room and an awning-covered terrace facing the water. The fan-cooled inner room has beige rattan peacock chairs and pale tablecloths and the Southeast Asian touches are reminders that the French were in Vietnam for many years. Vietnamese specialties include a delicious soup with shrimp and pineapple chunks, chicken curry and noodles with beef or chicken. Other specialties are French and include poulet chasseur (with onions and mushrooms) and boeuf bourguignon. Crêpes are among the desserts. There is a special three-course menu every night.

Le Santal By the Sea
Sandy Ground
☎ 590-87-53-48
Classic French
Dinner only
Very Expensive

Le Santal serves classic French cuisine in an attractive seaside restaurant near the Sandy Ground Bridge. It is in an unattractive residential area, but don't let the stray dogs, rusting cans and ramshackle houses dissuade you. When you cross the threshold, you'll be in a spotless white room with tables on the inner terrace. The outer one is right above the water. Sink into a brocade-covered chair and note the fine china and crystal and indirect lighting that gives the restaurant a warm glow.

The food is innovative and the menu changes frequently but always includes lots of salads, Norwegian salmon with chopped onion and egg, onion and asparagus soup and delicious hot and cold hors d'oeuvres. Main courses include duck with a variety of sauces, veal and lamb with red wine sauces and lobster soufflé. Crêpes Suzettes are a favorite dessert.

La Brasserie de la Gare
Port La Royale Marina
☎ 590-87-20-64
French/Italian
Open 11:30 am-10:30 pm
Inexpensive
This is the most popular restaurant at the Port La Royale, which is bustling from its 11:30 am opening till they pull the wicker chairs in at 10:30 pm. Tables are set on a roof-covered terrace and there are indoor tables as well. The inner rooms, with colorful finger paintings and TVs, are very popular with families.

回 **TIP**

The salads are enough for an entire meal, and two can share one with an omelette or a sandwich.

The menu, with both French and Italian specialties, is varied enough to appeal to all appetites. There are over 20 varieties of pizza. Toppings include onions, ham, sausage, pepperoni, seafood and mushrooms.

There are lots of pasta, fish dishes, beef and chicken dishes too. You can even enjoy a cheeseburger. The Brasserie looks out onto the water and, if it weren't for the 80☐ temperature, you'd be certain it was the Seine. Very informal.

Other Choices at the Marina

La Belle Epoque, ☎ 590-87-87-70, is Brasserie's neighbor on the marina promenade. Open for lunch and dinner, it has delicious thin-crust pizzas, burgers, salads and pastas. The dinner menu adds both French and Italian dishes. As with the other restaurants on the marina, there is an inner dining area and terrace tables. Check the posted menus to see which suits your appetite best.

La Main à la Pâté, ☎ 590-87-71-19. Try the house specialty, Salade Caraïbes, with fresh crabmeat, corn, peppers, escargot and greens. It makes a great lunch. There are a dozen varieties of pasta, crêpes with meats and cheese for a main course, pizzas, and sweets for dessert. Moderate.

Don Camillo da Enzo

Port La Royale Marina
☎ 590-87-52-88
Italian
Dinner only, 6:30-10:30 pm
Moderate

If you enjoy Italian food in informal surroundings, you'll enjoy Don Camillo, which is on the marina's outer walkway. It has two dining areas. The back room has yellow walls, mauve and white tablecloths and padded wooden booths and there are tables on the outer terrace as well. Beef carpaccio, Caesar salad or mozzarella and tomatoes with olive oil are fine starters, and the meat lasagne is thick with spices. Pollo capriccosa with tomatoes and cheese and the gnocchi are delicious. Italian pastries and fruit tarts are great finishers. The popular bar here is a local meeting place. One wall displays letters and card written to the restaurant by satisfied customers from all over the world.

Le Chanteclair

Port La Royale Marina
☎ 590-87-94-60
Moderate

In a sea of marina restaurants, Le Chanteclair stands out. A small bi-level eatery, its bright yellow chairs and multi-colored seat cushions are striking, as are the blue glass plates on each table. The menu here stands out as well, with traditional French specialties, rather than the eclectic menus of its neighbors. Stuffed rabbit, conch fricassée, duck, pâtés and classic Caesar salads are staples, and there are daily specials. Most popular is the "Lobster Menu," which starts with crispy lobster rolls, moves on to a half-avocado stuffed with lobster and a half-lobster with vegetables. Leave room for the warm brioche served with pecan ice cream, minced apples and pears, topped with a caramel sauce.

Le Bar de la Mer
Market Square
☎ 590-87-81-79
Eclectic Menu
Inexpensive

An island institution if you count the number of young locals wearing Le Bar's distinctive T-shirt, this place is noisy and fun to be in. The first level is virtually all bar and you have to elbow through the crowd to the second-level dining area. The menu, in French, English and Spanish, includes a dozen pizzas and they come topped with pepperoni, goat cheese, onions, anchovies, ham, and peppers, among other things. Burgers and club sandwiches, including a croque monsieur and a croque madame, are stuffed and look delicious. There are lots of salads and both beef and tuna tartare. Beef comes grilled as well. Most of your neighbors will be washing the food down with beer.

Le Bar's Caribbean BBQ is extremely popular. Served on the outer patio, it has grilled spiny lobsters, local snapper, huge shrimp, sirloin steaks and lamb chops, all delightfully marinated and cooked to your taste. A salad and baked potato are served with your meal. Barbecues are held nightly starting at 7 pm till the last coal dies at 11:30 pm. Reggae and calypso music in the market square is a bonus. This is a great place to meet people.

L'Arawak Café across the street is similar in style, with a bar on the first level and dining on the second floor and outer patio. The menu here is more French. It, too, draws a young lively crowd. ☎ 590-87-99-67.

Market Square

This was the setting for the big finish of the movie *Speed 2*. The studio constructed a new waterfront area with multi-colored pastel buildings and kiosks. Many of them remain and the result is an expanded waterfront with a larger craft, fruit and vegetable market and a score of small restaurants. These are Marigot's answer to Grand Case's lolos (beachfront shacks). They serve Creole dishes and are quite inexpensive so they are always crowded at lunch. Some serve breakfast, while others stay open until early evening. Judging by the number of locals waiting for a table, **Enochs Place** is the top spot. Look for the blue and white awning near the market. Lunch choices include Creole shrimp, curried goat and lobster dishes – but the menu changes daily. Inexpensive. No Credit Cards. Closed Sunday.

Le Charlois Grill

Rue Felix Eboue
☎ 590-87-93-19
Steakhouse
Moderate

Another branch is on Simpson Bay.

There are times when nothing but a juicy steak will do. If that mood comes over you while you are in Marigot, head to Le Charlois, owned by a local butcher. The restaurant has high wood booths lining each wall. Each has plush velvet seats and backs. The decorations are cowhides and horns, and the Angus beef steaks and the other grilled meats are delicious. Start with an endive salad or an avocado stuffed with crabmeat. You can have beef en brochette or lamb chops as well.

L'OiZeau Rare

At the Port
☎ 590-87-56-38
French/Asian
Moderate- Expensive

While other Creole buildings in Marigot have been restored, L'OiZeau is the only one in town that still looks like a *case*, a typical Creole house. You can see others in Orleans and Colombier. It is painted in a variety of pastel shades with yellow featured predominantly. It has the gingerbread trim on its long veranda and along the eaves of its colorful peaked roof. Palm trees surround the building and spraying fountains are lit at night. The French onion soup is exceptional and there are lots of delicious salads at lunch. Starched tablecloths and

Lunch 11:30-2:30; dinner 6-10:30.

Limoges china set the mood at night, when salmon carpaccio, lamb Provençal, duck with mango, crab rolls and sashimi tuna are menu highlights.

La Brasserie de Marigot
Rue Charles de Gaulle
☎ 590-87-94-43
French
Hours: 7 am to 10 pm
Inexpensive

A long block from the port, La Brasserie de Marigot has both the look and the menu of a Left Bank restaurant. It has round marble tables and wrought iron chairs in the inner dining areas and on the sidewalk. The walls are decorated with posters and paintings of Paris. It opens for breakfast at 7 am and doesn't close until 10 pm. Breakfast includes croissants, brioche and other breads served with jelly and butter. You can also order an omelette, which is served for lunch with ham, cheese, tomatoes, peppers and onions. Burgers, goat cheese and shrimp salads, and grilled fish are popular at lunch. Dinner finds hot lobster soup or gazpacho. Fish dishes include mahi mahi grilled with a vanilla or passion-fruit sauce. Roast chicken, steak tartare and London broil are also dinner suggestions. Parfaits and gâteaux are among the desserts. There is a full bar.

Sint Maarten/St. Martin

Thai Garden
Sandy Ground
☎ 590-87-88-44
Thai/Vietnamese
Moderate

You can't miss this restaurant on the Nettlé Bay road. Look for a pagoda with a large *garuda* (bird) over the front door. Buddhas and statues representing Thai gods are set in the beautifully landscaped gardens. The food served is Thai, Vietnamese and Japanese, and the menu has over 100 items from which to choose. There are fixed price menus as well. Japanese sashimi is excellent (the fish was caught just a few hours earlier). Other dishes include sugarcane-wrapped shrimp, steamed crabs with vermicelli, steamed fish curry with coconut milk and vermicelli with pork and shrimp. Meat dishes include Cantonese roast duck and sliced beef with mushrooms. There are many vegetarian dishes on the menu.

La Case Créole
Sandy Ground
☎ 590-87-28-45
Moderate
Creole

If you'd like to sample Creole specialties, this is a good place to start. In a colorful Creole house surrounded by a tropical garden, you can eat in one of two dining rooms. Each has pastel walls, red lacquered chairs and plaid tablecloths. The serving staff is dressed in traditional garb and the music sets the mood.

You can order such items as mango shrimp or conch with vanilla sauce from the à la carte menu. The restaurant opens at 6:30 pm. Closed Sundays.

> ### 🔲 TIP
>
> One way to taste a lot of dishes at La Case Créole is to order the Assiette Gourmande (Gourmet Platter), which includes grilled lobster, stuffed crab, Créole boudin, conch boudin, conch ke-bob, cod accras, shrimp accras, and stuffed christophene. Side dishes include yam purée, gi-romen purée, plantains, red beans and Créole rice.

Le Mini-Club
Blvd. du Front de Mer
☎ 590-87-50-69
Creole
Inexpensive

Le Mini-Club looks like a giant tree house. Perched on thick wooden beams and set amid towering palms, it is cooled by the breezes rolling in from Marigot Bay. It has weathered walls, a high beamed roof and lots of lush tropical plants to break the dining room into sections. Le Mini-Club was Marigot's first restaurant and remains a local favorite, especially on Wednesday and Saturday nights when they serve their Creole buffets. The long table is filled with lobsters, shrimp, and other seafood, and roasts of beef, lamb and pork are carved upon request. There are also salad fixings and fresh fruit. The price is right and it's very informal. There is an à la carte menu on other nights.

Sidewalk Cafés

Zee Best, rue de la Liberté, is owned by a young French-Canadian couple. They make great sandwiches, breakfasts and salads. Takeout is available for picnics.

Le Colibre Patisserie, rue Charles de Gaulle, serves the most delicious pastries as well as sandwiches and salads.

Le Saint Germain, Port La Royale Marina, opens at 7 am for breakfast and doesn't close until midnight. There is a good light menu and tables on the terrace.

Mentalo Snack Bar, rue Charles de Gaulle in Le Village Arcade, serves burgers, sandwiches and pastries.

Restaurants in or Near Grand Case

Le Tastevin
Blvd. de Grand Case
☎ 590-87-55-45
Lunch & dinner
Expensive-Very Expensive

The most elegant restaurant on the Grand Case strip, Le Tastevin is marked by striped green and white awnings. The tables, covered with deep blue tablecloths and encircled by high back rattan chairs, are set on the covered terrace on the beach side of the boulevard. There are beautiful flowers throughout, including some on each table. You can start light with a mixed salad with balsamic vinagrette dressing or the more filling lobster bisque. Main courses include fresh salmon with dill or grilled vegetables, seared tuna with pepper sauce or the duck breast with banana and lime sauce. Fabulous desserts include apple pie with red berry sauce and chocolate and praline mousse. Tastevin means "wine taster" and the wine list is terrific with a wide price range. Reservations for dinner are a must.

Sint Maarten/St. Martin

Fish Pot
Blvd. de Grand Case
☎ 590-87-50-88
Expensive
Lunch & dinner

An elegant restaurant with a magnificent view of Grand Case Beach and the sparkling lights of Anguilla in the distance, Fish Pot is set on a long terrace and has a veranda right above the sand. Tables set with deep blue cloths and grey and apricot china are quite eyecatching. An imaginative menu features seafood (but also includes duck and veal). Fish Pot serves a delicious Caesar and brie salad and sautéed shrimp for openers. Lobster with ginger and lemon sauce has a unique taste, as does the blackened sea bass. Caribbean fish soup with big chunks of fish and shellfish is served as an appetizer and as a main course. If you eat lightly, you'll have room for the chocolate mousse cake or fruit tart.

L'Escapade
Blvd de Grand Case
☎ 590-87-75-04
Dinner only
Expensive

One of the most attractive restaurants on restaurant row, L'Escapade's dining terrace sits just above the beach facing Anguilla. The deep green tablecloths are offset by white carved chairs and the tables are widely spaced for dining comfort. The cuisine is French, as are virtually all the restaurants here, but you'll find a lot of West Indian flavors and off-beat items as well. Starters include tasty lobster bisque or chilled gazpacho. The mussels with sweet peppers in a pesto sauce seem to be the most popular dish, judging by the bowls of empty shells on lots of tables. The duck breast was served with a vegetable thyme sauce that had eggplant, zucchini and peppers in it. Rack of lamb and a napoleon of mahi-mahi were excellent. Bananas flambée with rum sauce makes a delicious dessert. There's music at dinner most evenings.

Rainbow
Blvd. de Grand Case
☎ 590-87-55-80
Nouvelle French
Dinner only; closed Sunday
Expensive
An attractive choice for dinner, Rainbow's split-level dining room with white beamed ceiling and walls, and blue and white checkered tablecloths, has a jaunty nautical look that is augmented by the sound of the waves just a few feet away. The menu at Rainbow is very innovative and has dishes not served elsewhere on the island. Among them is a shrimp and scallop fricassée, warm duck salad with fried onions, and bell peppers stuffed with lobster. You'll also find veal scaloppine with capers and filet of red snapper with a parmesan crust. Great desserts include honey, orange and ginger soufflés and profiteroles.

Il Nettuno

Blvd. de Grand Case

☎ 590-87-77-88

Dinner 6-10:30 pm

Moderate

A delightful surprise on this street with so many French restaurants, Il Nettuno is an Italian establishment, and a very good one, too. You'll notice the opera music as you step over the threshold. The green tiled bar is popular with people waiting for tables and others enjoying a drink at waterside. Graceful archways separate the bar area from the dining rooms where the tables are covered with pink cloths and floral napkins. A floral centerpiece marks the antipasto table that is covered with cheeses, marinated vegetables and cold meats. Start with the fiore de carpaccio salmon and calamari or the fresh mussels in a garlic tomato sauce. Homemade pasta, the house specialty, is served with a multitude of sauces. Ravioli with smoked salmon and veal scaloppine with porcini mushrooms are customer favorites.

L'Auberge Gourmande

Blvd. de Grand Case

☎ 590-87-73-37

Moderate

Closed Wednesdays

The sturdy walls of this unusual stone *case* remained unscathed by the winds of Hurricane Luis. Not in typical Creole style, the house lacks a terrace and gingerbread trim, but instead has a covered stone patio and graceful archways that separate one dining area from the next. The frequently changing menu is primarily Nouvelle French. The evening specials are posted on a blackboard on the patio. Among the dishes often served are lamb chops with fines herbes, duck breast with honey and lemon, and chicken breast with apples. Other dishes include escargots and foie gras. This is an informal choice with unhurried service and a friendly staff.

Hevea

Blvd. de Grand Case
☎ 590-87-56-85
Expensive
Dinner Only

A tiny gem with less than a dozen tables, Hevea occupies the front rooms of a restored Creole mansion. Everything about the restaurant points to the owner's good taste. The walls are white and so are the hand-embroidered place mats at each setting. The floral china and plush red-cushioned armchairs give the dining areas a provincial look. The cuisine is delightfully French. Lobster bisque or grilled prawns are delicious starters. Main courses include duck with Madeira sauce, filet de boeuf in cognac, and the Duet, which is mahi mahi and smoked salmon. Leave room for the bananas flambées with rum or the chocolate delight with coffee cream. There is a pianist or a singer during dinner. Reservations are a must.

Sint Maarten/St. Martin

Closed Sept.

Le Pressoir
Blvd. de Grand Case
☎ 590-87-76-62
Moderate
French/Creole
Closed Tuesdays

One of the oldest Creole houses in Grand Case is home to Le Pressoir, a French restaurant with lots of Creole touches. Look for the iron "pressoir" at the door and park across the street. Salt mining was what first attracted settlers to St. Martin and this pressoir was originally used for refining the salt. The dining rooms, separated by curved archways, have apricot walls trimmed with lavender to match the wood beams on the ceiling and the window shutters. Tables covered with floral cloths add to the feeling that you're eating in a giant dollhouse. Don't miss the delicious onion-asparagus tart. Main courses include roast lamb with tropical fruit, sautéed sole with apples, pastas and roast duck. Desserts are a must here. White chocolate mousse with cherries and hot chocolate mousse cake are at the top of everyone's list.

The Lolos of Grand Case

"Lolos" were the beach shacks that once dotted Grand Case Beach. Typically made of wood with thatched roofs, they were no match for the winds of Hurricane Luis and many were not rebuilt after it hit. But a few more sturdy structures have reappeared here and on Friar's Beach nearby. Lolos serve barbecued spare ribs, chicken and lobster with johnnycakes, plantains and rice and beans. **La Case à Rhums** and **Chez Cheryl** each have a handful of tables. You can eat on the beach or take the food back to your room. It's finger lickin' good.

Bombay Brasserie
Blvd. de Grand Case
☎ 590-29-67-20
Moderate

One of Grand Case's newest restaurants, the unpretentious Bombay Brasserie is unique on a street where fabulous restaurants serve variations of French cuisine. With a pitched red roof, whitewashed walls and blue trim, this small cottage looks American, but the aroma of curry tells you that it's an Indian restaurant. The specialties are dishes prepared in their tandoor (clay oven). These include chicken and beef. There are lots of vegetarian choices as well. Everything is served with rice.

Dining Farther North

Captain Oliver's

Oyster Pond
☎ 590-87-30-00
Moderate

Captain Oliver's resort sits on the French-Dutch border on beautiful Oyster Pond, a secluded cove on the island's eastern shore. In fact, the resort is on French soil, while the restaurant, built on wooden planks, is over Dutch waters. The terrace is open-sided but covered with white sailcloth and diners can watch the sailboats and yachts moving through the canal to the marina. Captain Oliver was a top restaurateur in Paris before building his hideaway here about 20 years ago. His goal was to provide good food and service at a moderate price. He has succeeded.

The restaurant opens from 7 to 10:30 am for breakfast that includes a buffet. Reopening at noon, the lunch buffet and à la carte menu is served until 5 pm. The buffet has cold fish and meats, hot soups, salads and great desserts. Salads, burgers and sandwiches dominate the à la carte menu. At 5 pm the staff starts to set the tables for dinner with blue and white table cloths, lighted hurricane lamps, and more formal china and glassware. The dinner menu reflects Captain Oliver's roots, blending pastas and fried chicken with superbly cooked seafood, including lobsters from the tank prepared in a variety of ways. A cold appetizer called Ile Coco Captain Oliver is sliced raw tuna in olive oil and a hot pepper sauce with coconut and lemon. It will please those who like sushi. Palm and avocado salad, stuffed crabs, Creole-style grouper and fine veal and duck dishes are other choices. The restaurant serves till 11 pm, although the bar stays open later.

Chez Yvette
Orleans, French Quarter
☎ 590-87-32-03
Inexpensive-Moderate

There are many family-run restaurants like Chez Yvette in the British Virgin Islands, but they are a rarity here. The restaurant, in a small white, pink and green *case* with gingerbread trim, sits in a small garden just off the main road in Orleans. Eating dinner here is like being invited to someone's home – only the food is better. There are only 10 tables, each one covered in a bright red cloth with fresh flowers on top. The restaurant was named for its owner/chef, Yvette, who, sadly, has passed away. Her family continues to run the restaurant and little has changed. The freshest ingredients at the market are purchased each morning and then the day's menu is planned. They cook "to the house," so you must have a reservation. The Creole dishes are prepared just as they would be in kitchens on the island. There is no overlay of French food. Chez Yvette's favorites include salt fish cakes, spicy fish fritters (accras), spareribs, and conch and

Closed Wednesday.

Chez Yvette does not accept credit cards.

dumplings. Stews prepared with lobster, conch, chicken or pork chops are very popular. Vegetables and rice and peas are served with each main course. There are always soups and salads too. Yvette's daughter greets all her guests and is very friendly. Your evening here will be an enjoyable one.

Poulet d'Orléans

Orléans French Quarter

☎ 590-87-48-24

Inexpensive

Closed Monday.

For the previous edition of this guide our St. Martin friends told us that Chez Yvette (above) served the most authentic Creole food on the island. According to these same "mavens," Poulet d'Orléans, not far from Chez Yvette, is equally good and the ambience is more interesting. It's set in an original "case" (traditional house) that is over 100 years old and you'll immediately notice the intricate gingerbread fretwork. The house is filled with antiques and collectibles, some of them for sale. It looks out over the valley and rolling hills nearby. Tony, the owner/chef, and his four delightful children make diners feel like old friends. The menu, which changes daily, is virtually identical to Yvette's, since both serve what is fresh and available at the market that day. The "don't-miss" dish here is the spareribs. They're finger-lickin' good.

Dinner only. No credit cards.

L'Astrolabe
Esmeralda Resort
Orient Bay
☎ 590-87-36-36
Moderate
Closed Wednesdays

In its own building near the gate of this villa community, L'Astrolabe serves both breakfast and dinner. It is quite elegant inside, resembling a French restaurant in Nice, and has brown tile floors, pale posts that support the beamed ceiling (dividing the dining room into areas) and lots of prints and posters on the walls. The inner dining area is fan-cooled and there are tables on the terrace as well. The terrace is in a garden setting in the rear of the house. Comfortable, it has high-backed armchairs and widely spaced tables set with fine crystal and china. The menu changes daily. A recent menu had sliced smoked salmon and lobster bisque for starters and many fish dishes, including jumbo shrimp with chutney and grilled mahi mahi with zucchini. The filet of beef with mushrooms was served in a puff pastry shell. There was a choice of desserts. Drive by early in the day or call to check on the menu before making reservations.

Jade Garden Restaurant
Oyster Bay Resort
☎ 590-543-6040
Moderate

There are only a handful of restaurants in the Oyster Bay-Dawn Beach area and most are

Lunch 12-3:30; dinner 6-11.

small beach shacks serving barbecued foods. Jade Garden, in the Oyster Bay Resort (but independently owned), serves the island's best Cantonese food. The setting on the resort's open-air terrace overlooking the bay, is delightful as well. There is also an indoor dining area. All the typical dishes are served, including spareribs, spring rolls, sweet and sour chicken, beef or shrimp with broccoli, beef or chicken in black bean or curry sauce and several stir-fry dishes as well. For those who prefer pastas or burgers, they are on a separate menu, along with lobster dishes and main course salads.

Dining in or Near Philipsburg

L'Escargot
Front Street, Philipsburg
☎ 599-542-2483
Lunch & dinner
Expensive

It's a surprise to find that one of the island's top French restaurants is on the Dutch side of the island. But you know L'Escargot is first-rate because it's been here for over 30 years. You can't miss the landmark 19th-century house on Front Street painted in red, white and blue with a long wrap-around veranda and lots of gingerbread trim. There are no subtle decorative touches inside either. The small dining areas have pink walls decorated with murals of France inspired by Toulouse Lautrec and lots of colorful posters. Other walls have hundreds of business cards from satisfied guests and requests for L'Escargot recipes. Escargots are the house specialty and are prepared with wild mushrooms and shallots, in cherry tomatoes and garlic butter, baked in garlic in pots or in an omelette. If snails aren't your favorite thing, you can start with frogs' legs, crêpes filled with caviar or shrimp ravioli in lobster sauce. Main courses include shrimp in cognac and garlic butter, poached salmon in herb sauce or chicken breast with mango dressing. Crème brûlée and chocolate mousse are among the desserts.

Antoine's

119 Front Street, Philipsburg
☎ 599-542-2690
Expensive

Dinner 6-10.

Antoine's looks out onto Great Bay, so ask for a table on the covered terrace. The dinner menu is continental, serving French, Italian and some Creole dishes. Antoine's is quite elegant, with blue and white crisp cloths, candles on each table and impeccable service. The fish or French onion soup are delicious starters and if you like pâté, you'll like it here. Red snapper with wine and lemon sauce was a light entrée, while the duck with cherry brandy sauce was more filling. Lobster dishes are always a good choice. The lunch menu is unexceptional, but the soups, salads and sandwiches are freshly prepared and attractively presented.

The Wajang Doll
Front Street, Philipsburg
☎ 599-542-2687
Moderate

While there are no Dutch restaurants on Sint Maarten, there are a number of Indonesian (formerly Dutch East Indies) restaurants that serve the traditional *rijsttafel*. Translated as "rice table," it is an Indonesian smorgasbord that starts with rice and 20 or more dishes eaten with it. Dishes include meats, vegetables and fruits. The à la carte menu includes *saté udang*, which is marinated shrimp kebabs with peanut sauce, and *sup jawa*, a soup with rice noodles and spicy meatballs. A *wajang* doll is a prop used in Indonesian folklore plays. Ask for a table in the garden of this brown and yellow West Indian house near Old Street.

Old Captain
Front Street, Philipsburg
☎ 599-542-6988
Moderate

An island of Chinese and Japanese fare in a sea of French restaurants, Old Captain is an attractive port of call. Its pink and black onyx dining room with colorful aquariums and its narrow terrace offer a respite from bustling Front Street. The sushi bar is the restaurant's most popular stop. And why not? The yellowtail tuna and wahoo came from this morning's catch. They and other fish are served as sushi, sashimi, temaki and norimaki. Other Japanese foods, such as teriyaki with beef, chicken and shrimp, are also served. The large Chinese menu includes stir-fries, curries and lots of vegetarian dishes.

Kangaroo Court
Hendrick's Straat (alley adjoining Court House)
☎ 599-542-4278
Inexpensive
Because the local market creates a traffic jam, both for autos and pedestrians, on this narrow street, it is very easy to walk right by this unassuming deli. It's a hang-out for those working at the court and in the shops nearby. It serves breakfast from 7:30 until 11 am and then lunch till 3. The black stone walls are very old but they have been decorated with vivid colors and wall hangings from other Caribbean islands. Head past the few tables in the front room (but pause to check out the fresh pastries and sandwiches), then into the cool inner courtyard. Egg dishes, pancakes, French toast and bagels are served for breakfast, along with the pastries. Sandwiches, with bread baked on the premises, include tuna, chicken, shrimp salad, roast beef and turkey. Giant salad bowls have grilled chicken as well. The day's specials are on a bulletin board and there is a menu. Take-out is very popular here. Some items are already packaged; others are prepared while you wait.

Deli / café.
Closes at 5 pm.

Sint Maarten/St. Martin

Spartaco

Almond Grove, Cole Bay
☎ 599-544-5379
Expensive

Floodlights allow this beautiful 200-year-old
stone plantation house to shine even at night.
The restored estate has magnificent gardens
with palm trees, flowering plants and marble
statues. Spartaco serves Northern Italian food
and imports many of the ingredients from Italy.
All the pastas and the olive oil are made in-
house. House specialties include grilled
radicchio in onion and caper vinaigrette, mussels sautéed in garlic and black angel hair
pasta sautéed with shrimp and artichoke. Veal
Vesuviana with mozzarella and tomatoes and
rack of lamb are good choices. Tiramisu and ter-
rine of chocolate are great finishers but you
might prefer dessert and after-dinner drinks in
the Spartaco Cigar Bar, where jazz and classical music is live from 11 pm to 2 am.

Mark's Place

Food Center, Cole Bay
☎ 599-543-2625
Inexpensive-Moderate

Lunch & dinner.

Closed Sunday and Monday.

We remembered Mark's Place from previous
trips to St. Martin, when it was an informal bistro on the Orient Beach Road. It was not there
when we returned to prepare this new edition,
but we were delighted to stumble over it in its
new location near Spartaco Restaurant. Still
informal and still serving huge portions of Cre-

ole specialties and fresh seafood, it seems to be going strong. Daily specials are posted on the blackboard.

Dining in or Near Maho

La Rosa Too
Maho Village
☎ 599-545-3470
Moderate

In a quiet corner of the Maho Complex, La Rosa Too's customers are primarily people who live or winter on the island. Table talk, all in English, revolves around golf scores, bridge games and the latest gossip. The owners are very gregarious and welcoming – and the kitchen prepares delicious Italian dishes. The menu is very large and items are prepared to order, so have a drink at the bar while waiting for your table. Starters include beef and salmon carpaccio and steamed clams, and there are lots of pasta dishes that can be ordered in half-portions. Chicken is prepared piccata and parmigiana, veal comes Milanese-style or with peppers, and the osso buco is served with gnocchi. There are small dining areas set off by glass walls. Tables can be close when the restaurant is crowded.

Dinner only, until 11 pm.

Closed Tuesday.

◙ TIP

There are two pizza places in the complex as well. **Mamma Mia's**, ☎ 599-545-3934, is on the second level of the hotel, while **Pizza Pasta**, ☎ 599-545-4034, is behind the casino.

Citrus (and Market)
Cupecoy Bay
☎ 599-545-4343
Expensive

This is a delightful choice in an area where there are few restaurants. It shares a small shopping strip near the entrance to the beach with a gourmet take-out shop called Market (same owners). The indoor dining room is quite formal, with red velvet chairs and striking oil paintings. There are several dining levels, all dimly lit and inviting. The menu changes frequently to take advantage of the freshest ingredients, but a recent menu had these starters: asparagus soup with crabmeat, seared ahi tuna and sushi rolls served with seaweed salad. Main courses included poached lobster tail, roasted veal chop with shallots and mushrooms and pan-roasted duck served with artichokes and potatoes. There is also a dessert menu and a good wine list.

Closed Wednesdays.

Market, open daily from 7:30-7, has a daily selection of meat, fish and vegetable salads, sandwiches, quiches, fresh bread, frozen foods, fresh fruit and wines. It's a great place to get picnic lunches.

▣ TIP

Citrus is a short stroll from the Atlantis Casino. There are interesting restaurants there, which we've detailed in the *After Dark* section, pages 266-67.

Cheri's Café

Maho Village
☎ 599-545-3361
Inexpensive-Moderate

Informal and with lots of options, Cheri's Café is the busiest restaurant on the island. The covered circular terrace is set with umbrella-covered tables and multi-colored director's chairs. Cheri's opens for lunch at 11 am and serves until midnight. The live music starts at 8 pm. Salads come with tuna, sardines or turkey and the burgers with cheese, onion or bacon. There are super-size sandwiches and spaghetti with meat, shrimp or garlic butter sauce. You can eat light, but there's also steak and shrimp or steak and lobster combos, tuna and shrimp brochettes and pasta specials, like lasagne. There is a menu for kids under 12.

Cheri's does not take reservations.

Paris Bistro

Maho Plaza
☎ 599-545-5677

A popular dining spot overlooking Maho's main street, the bistro is small and the dozen tables

Sint Maarten/St. Martin

have yellow checked cloths and colorful flowers. Starters include fried calamari, eggplant caviar, smoked salmon and foie gras. There are always pastas, served with pesto, marinara or primavera sauces. Lobster tails and beef brochettes are well prepared. To sample a variety of dishes, ask for the gourmet tasting menu. Try the crêpe suzettes before heading to the casino across the street.

Dining in Simpson Bay

Mezzanotte
Simpson Bay
☎ 599-544-2236
Moderate

If you enjoy your Italian food with the hearty red sauces favored in Sicily and Southern Italy, head to Mezzanotte on Simpson Bay. Many of their seafood and pasta dishes are served with spicy sauce. It's in an attractive spot adjoining the lagoon. You can opt for a table on the covered porch near the bar or in the larger indoor dining room. Indirect lighting, high-backed carved wooden chairs with colorfully embroidered pillows and flowers everywhere give the restaurant an inviting ambience. The menu is very large, with 20 pasta dishes and an equal number of meat, poultry and seafood specials. Among the pastas are lasagna, penne with sausage and mushrooms and linguine with mussels and clams. Veal scaloppine, chicken with eggplant and lobster fra diavolo are also specials. If your dining partner prefers food without sauce, there is an extensive grill menu as well.

Ric's American Sports Bar

Airport Road, Simpson Bay
☎ 599-545-3630
Inexpensive

Ric's has moved from its Front Street location to new digs right on the bay. In fact, you can sit at a table on the restaurant's back terrace and see the water. We miss the "old" Ric's that looked like a bar in a college town with pennants of sports teams for décor. The new Ric's hasn't settled into its skin yet, but the large-screen TV and smaller sets throughout are still tuned to major sports events or video reruns of them. The menu still has burgers, hot dogs and subs but is heavier now on Tex-Mex items such as taco salad and chili con carne. There are at least a dozen brews – several on tap.

> ### 🔲 NOTE
> Ric's old spot at #69 Front Street is under new management but the décor and menu remain the same as before.

Rancho Steak House

Airport Road, Simpson Bay
☎ 599-545-2495
Moderate

St. Martin has excellent steak houses, on both the French and Dutch sides of the island, but as

far as we can tell Rancho is the only one that
serves Argentine-style meats. That means the
meats are cooked over open fires and are specific cuts of beef. The *parrillada* consists of several kinds of beef, plus innards and sausages.
Served on a small stove designed to keep items
hot until eaten, it is an Argentine specialty.
Other traditional steaks include churrasco,
entrecôte and lomo. Tomato-onion salad is the
favored side-dish and the French-fried potatoes
are the perfect vegetable. There are chicken,
lamb and fish dishes, too. It's a huge restaurant
sitting on the bay, with dining areas surrounded by greenery. The menu is virtually
identical at lunch and dinner.

▣ TIP

If you prefer a traditional steak
house, a branch of **Le
Charlois**, the Marigot steakhouse, is nearby as well. ☎ 599-
544-5531.

The Boathouse Restaurant

Simpson Bay
☎ 599-544-5409
Inexpensive

An anchored boat decorated with flags and
mermaids at Simpson Bay Lagoon serves as
The Boathouse Restaurant. The rectangular
bar is a popular local hangout and is quite
crowded at happy hour. Since The Boathouse
serves breakfast, lunch and dinner, it is always
bustling. You can enjoy eggs, pancakes and

omelettes at breakfast (7:30 to 10:30 am), followed by salads, sandwiches, burgers and pastas for lunch (11:30 am to 2:30 pm). Dinner,
which is served until 10 pm, has a conch cocktail or peel n' eat shrimp, seafood kebabs, surf 'n
turf, and filet mignon. On Friday evenings a
rock group entertains. You can head to the
adjacent News Café after dinner. On Sundays
they serve dinner only.

★ NOTE

Chesterfields, Great Bay
Marina, Philipsburg, has the
same menu, same ambience and
same owners as The Boathouse.

After Dark

The days are hardly long enough to
squeeze in all the things you want to do,
so after-dark action on the island is low key
and filled with very good food, island music,
piano bars, theme nights and casino chips.
Check the newspaper or ask your concierge
about events during your stay. Always call
clubs before starting out. Hot spots never last
long.

Sint Maarten/St. Martin

Maho Plaza

A lively nighttime destination with a score of restaurants, a casino, comedy club and theater. **Cheri's Café**, a covered terrace restaurant, has live music every night from 8 pm to 1 am. You can have just drinks or dine there.

Theater closed Sundays.

The **Casino Royale Theater** (☎ 599-545-2590) has Las Vegas-style revues, concerts and shows with both local and imported acts. Showtime is 9:30 nightly in season. The **Q discotheque** opens at 10 pm. ☎ 599-545-2632.

Mullet/Cupecoy Bay

The **Atlantis World Casino** (☎ 599-545-4601), which is open and bustling 24/7, is surrounded by seven restaurants. Options range from Moroccan to sushi and from formal (long pants) to informal (shorts acceptable). The most interesting eatery is **Casablanca** (☎ 590-27-49-87), the Moroccan restaurant, serving dinner-only from 7 nightly (closed Monday). You'll enjoy the tajines (stews) with lamb, chicken, sausages or beef. The sauce is sweetened with raisins and almonds. Start with the traditional *messe* (antipasto) that includes seven salads and several condiments. You can sample each. Salads include tomato and onion, potato, eggplant and peppers.

Le Montmart, ☎ 599-545-39-39, serves French food, including mussels, choucroute and cassoulets. **Sitar** (Indian fare), **Ferrari** (Italian) and **Asian Sushi Bar** are the other dinner-only options. **The Sugar Cane Café** and **Bella Napoli Pizzeria** serve from early morning till 1 am daily.

Marigot

Head to **Port La Royale**, where the walkways adjoining the marina house a dozen restaurants – some gourmet and some informal – serving everything from French food to pizza. All the restaurants have indoor and terrace dining and menus are posted. They are crowded well into the night. We've detailed some of the restaurants above, but you can come for a nightcap and the live music, too.

Thursday nights are special, with local bands and street entertainers performing on the promenade starting at 7 pm. The music ranges from reggae to jazz. The shops stay open late as well. But things have a way of changing here without notice, so you should check in advance to make sure of the schedule.

There are a score of discos and nightclubs in Marigot. We've detailed them on pages 270-71.

Another nighttime center, **Market Square**, is two blocks away, on the dock. There are some gourmet restaurants here, but there are many more informal cafés with patios that serve Creole food, including barbecued ribs and chicken. There's live calypso and reggae music nightly in the plaza. The market stays open late on Wednesday evenings.

The most popular café, **Le Bar de la Mer** (page 236), doesn't take reservations, so expect to wait for a table. **La Vie en Rose** (page 231) at the edge of the plaza has a sidewalk café where they serve French pastries long after the restaurant has closed.

Arawak Café is also popular.

Orient Beach

Popular during the day, the beachfront restaurants here are also open and alive well into the night. Informal but not shacks, these restaurants have both indoor and outdoor dining areas. The diners are a good mix of locals and visitors, and the restaurants are noisy and full of fun. The food served varies from Spanish tapas to pizza to French fare. Check posted menus. Bikini Beach, Kakao, Kon-Tiki, Coco Beach and Waikiki each has a private parking area. You can walk from one to the other. Noted for their beach parties and live bands, they draw young people.

Reservations are not necessary at the beach places.

Casinos

All the casinos on the island are on the Dutch side of the border. Most are in hotel complexes, but there are a few in Philipsburg too. They all have slot machines, blackjack, roulette and craps. Some have stud poker, while others offer betting on horseraces and sports events. They include: **Casino Royale** (Maho), **Lightning** (Simpson Bay), **Rouge et Noir** and the **Coliseum** (both on Front Street, Philipsburg), **Great Bay Casino** (Great Bay Hotel, Philipsburg), **Pelican Casino** (Pelican Hotel, Simpson Bay), **Atlantis Casino** (Cupecoy Bay) and **Princess Port de Plaisance Casino** (Cole Bay).

You must be at least18 to gamble.

Calypso/Reggae

Bamboo Bernies - Caravanserai Resort (Maho), ☎ 599-545-3622, is a "destination" for daytime and nighttime fun. It serves sushi as well as BBQ ribs. It has both a volleyball court and a cinema on its beach. Music every night, from reggae to funk and blues.

Kali's Beach Bar - Friar's Bay, ☎ 590-51-07-44, is a ramshackle spot with excellent BBQ, cool drinks and the best reggae bands on the island. Ask about Kali's "Full Moon" party.

Everyt'ing Cool, ☎ 599-542-2483, and **The Reggae Café** (no phone), both in Philipsburg, are local spots where the calypso and reggae go non-stop.

La Samanna (☎ 590-87-64-00), **Panoramic Privilege** (☎ 590-87-38-38), **La Belle Créole** (☎ 590-87-66-00), **Oyster Bay Beach Hotel** (☎ 599-52-2206) are other options.

Jazz & Other Music

French Side

Le Cohibar, Nettlé Bay (☎ 590-29-65-22), is the hottest nightspot on the island. Elegant furnishings, good music, liquors and cigars. Opens at 10 pm.

Havana Too, Front de Mer, Marigot (☎ 590-53-64-32), has an outer terrace for light foods and drinks. There is a pool. Furniture is Salvation Army-style. The indoor dance floor has live music and theme nights.

L'Alibi, Auberge de Mer, Marigot (☎ 590-87-08-39), is a popular discotheque that has theme nights.

L'Inédit, rue Victor Maurasse, Marigot (☎ 590-87-28-26), serves an eclectic menu and has lively cabaret revues.

Chili's Café, Sandy Ground (☎ 590-29-38-08), serves Tex-Mex foods as well as tapas. Live music nightly. Chili's has a great location on Marigot's only beach.

Bodeguita del Medio, Auberge del Mer, Marigot (☎ 590-87-98-41), is the island's only Latin/Cuban club.

Club Pasha, Front de Mer, Marigot (☎ 590-87-95-77), overlooks Market Square. It's a lively discotheque.

Coco Club, Grand Case (☎ 590-51-91-04), is the most popular club in this small town. Its champagne parties and theme nights draw large crowds.

Boo Boo Jam's Beach Party, Orient Beach (☎ 590-87-03-13), is a Friday night "must."

Follow Me, Marigot, is a piano bar at the new West Indies shopping center.

Dutch Side

Sopranos Piano Bar, Maho (☎ 599-522-7088), is a dimly lit, comfortable bar with live piano music.

Sunset Beach Bar, Caravanserai Resort, Maho (☎ 599-545-3998), is an open-air bar that draws throngs of imbibers who head there for happy hour and return late in the evenings for the live music.

Bliss, Caravanserai Resort, Maho (☎ 599-545-3996), offers martini soirées, international theme nights and a unique open-air nightclub where you can dance to local bands.

The Greenhouse, Bobby's Marina, Philipsburg (☎ 599-542-2941) and **The Boat House**, Simpson Bay (☎ 599-544-5409), share informal menus, a comfortable ambience and live music. Check on schedules.

Spartaco Wine Bar, Almond Grove, Cole Bay (☎ 599-544-5379), features jazz, popular and classical music, along with fine wines, liquors and cigars.

Peg Leg Pub, Three Palms Plaza, Simpson Bay (☎ 599-577-1726), has a 30-foot bar, cable TVs and over 30 varieties of beer.

Tango Sunset Dinner Cruise has a Creole buffet, open bar and good music. Call ☎ 599-544-2640 to check current schedules and departure points.

St. Martin A to Z

ATMs

There are ATMs in Philipsburg, Maho and at the airport.

Banks

Barclay's Bank, Philipsburg and Simpson Bay. Hours: 8:30 am-3 pm, Monday through Friday.

Banque des Antilles Françaises (BDAF), Marigot. Hours: 8 am to noon and 2 to 3:30 pm, Monday through Friday.

Cinemas

Sandy Ground Cinema, Sandy Ground, just outside of Marigot, ☎ 590-51-07-60. French language or subtitles.

Sunset Theater, Simpson Bay, ☎ 599-544-3630.

Climate

Sunny and warm year-round. Average temperature is 80□F. Constant trade winds moderate the temperature.

Clothing

Informal is the key word. Casual chic attire is the norm at the better restaurants, but shorts are accepted in the casinos and moderate restaurants. Jackets are rare. No ties.

Currency Exchange

Change Caraïbes, rue Charles de Gaulle, Marigot.

Departure Tax

Passengers departing on international flights from Princess Juliana Airport must pay a $20 departure tax. The inter-island departure tax is $6. All taxes are included in the ticket price on the French side.

Electric Current

Dutch Side - 110V, the same as in the United States. No converters or adapters are required.

French Side - 220V. Requires a converter and French adapter plug.

Emergency Numbers

French Side: **Police**, ☎ 590-87-50-10; **Hospital**, ☎ 87-50-07.

Dutch Side: **Police**, ☎ 111; **Hospital**, ☎ 599-543-1111.

Holidays

Contact tourist offices, listed below, for details.

January 6 – **Epiphany** (French side). Dining, dancing and observing the ancient French custom of serving *galette des rois* (Kings' Cake).

February (date varies) – French **Carnival** is a pre-Lenten celebration that lasts till Ash Wednesday. Parties, parades and a Carnival Queen are part of the celebration.

March (date varies) – Sint Maarten's **Heineken Regatta** is a well-attended sailing race with entrants from all over the Caribbean.

April (date varies) – The Dutch **Carnival** celebration lasts two weeks. A Carnival King and Queen are elected and there are parades. Events are held at the Carnival Village in Philipsburg.

May 30 – Dutch Sint Maarten celebrates the **Queen's birthday** with fireworks.

July 14 – French St. Martin celebrates **Bastille Day** (Independence Day) with parades and fireworks.

November 11 – **St. Martin's Day** celebrates the signing of the treaty that divided the island with ceremonies held at the marker on Terres Basses/Cupecoy Beach.

Internet Access

Parcel Plus at Wathy Square and in Simpson Bay has computers for customer use.

Marinas

French Side - **Captain Oliver's**, Oyster Road, ☎ 590-87-33-47; **Port de Lonvilliers**, Anse Marcel, ☎ 590-87-31-94.

Dutch Side - **Bobby's Marina**, Philipsburg, ☎ 599-542-2366; **Simpson Bay Yacht Club**, Simpson Bay, ☎ 599-544-2309.

Mini-Golf

There is bowling and a mini-golf course at the **Howell Center** in Marigot. Hours: 10 am to 10 pm, Monday through Saturday.

Newspapers

The Miami Herald, USA Today and The New York Times are sold in Maho Bay and Nettlé Bay Shopping Strip.

Local papers include *The News,* in French, and *The Herald*, in English.

Personal Safety

Use the same common sense you would at home.

⊚ Don't flash money or wear expensive jewelry.

⊚ Avoid areas that are dark after business hours.

- Do not leave valuables in your car overnight, even if the car is locked.

- Lock your car at the beach.

Photo Express

Marina Photo at Port La Royale, Marigot. ☎ 590-87-88-18.

Pharmacy

Pharmacy Caraïbes, Anse Marcel Rd. Open 8 am-10:30 pm. Closed Sunday.

Prescription Drugs

Bring enough drugs to last your entire trip. Over-the-counter items are readily available.

Physicians

Should you need a doctor, ask your concierge to recommend one or to contact one for you. There are dentists and doctors with a wide variety of specialties on the island.

Population

There are approximately 30,000 people living in Saint Martin and 33,000 in Sint Maarten.

Post Office

Dutch Side - Philipsburg.

French Side - Marigot, Grand Case, Orléans.

Religious Institutions

There are Anglican, Baptist, Catholic, Latter Day Saints, Methodists, Jehovah's Witnesses and Seventh Day Adventist churches (with some on both sides of the island). Jewish services are held during the High Holy Days.

Telephones

Area Codes: French St. Martin, 590; Dutch Sint Maarten, 599.

On-Island Calls: To call the French side from the Dutch side, dial 00-590-590 + six-digit number.

To call the Dutch side from the French side, dial 1-599 + seven-digit number.

Credit Card Calls from public phones: From the French side, dial 19-00-11 (requires deposit). From the Dutch side, dial 001-800-872-2881. You will be connected to AT&T.

Local Calls from Public Phones: French St. Martin requires a France Telecom Card that can be purchased in a post office. No coins are accepted.

Dutch Sint Maarten requires a Netherlands Antilles Telecom Card, which you can buy at the post office.

Time Zone

When the eastern coast of the United States is on Eastern Standard Time, the time in St. Martin is plus one hour. During Daylight Savings Time, the times are exactly the same. The French side uses the 24-hour clock.

Tourist Offices

St. Martin: **Bureau d'Office du Tourism**, Marigot Port, ☎ 590-87-57-23. Hours: Monday through Friday, 8:30 am to 1 pm and 2:30 to 5:30 pm. Saturday, 8 am to noon.

Sint Maarten: **Vineyard Park Office**, ☎ 599-542-2337. Hours: Monday through Friday, 8 am to noon, 1 to 5 pm. Closed Saturday and Sunday.

Anguilla

A Daytrip or Weekend Getaway

Eating dinner at a restaurant in Marigot's Market Square or in one along Grand Case Beach, you'll notice twinkling lights on the horizon. It's Anguilla, five miles north of St. Martin and the most northerly of the Leeward Islands. One of the few islands not named by Columbus, Anguilla is 16 miles long and three miles wide. The long narrow shape may be responsible for its name – "anguilla" is the French word for eel. Only slightly smaller than St. Martin/Sint Maarten, Anguilla has only 12,000 citizens. The island is quite flat. Its highest point is Crocus Hill, 213 feet above sea level. It is also very dry and, like St. Barts, it has no rivers or streams. This made it difficult to grow sugar or cotton, so the few plantations that were built failed and few slaves were brought to Anguilla.

The earliest colonists were British, from St. Christopher (St. Kitts), 70 miles southeast. St. Kitts was Britain's most important colony in the Caribbean. Anguilla was twice attacked by the French – the last time in 1796 – but English frigates arrived in time to defend the island. In 1688, a group of Irish sailors came to the island. Their descendants are clustered in Island Harbour. The island's population is predominantly of African descent. Without agriculture, Anguillans turned to the sea and eked out livings as fishermen and boat-builders.

★ DID YOU KNOW?

The island's national sport is not cricket, but boat racing.

An incident in the 1960's brought Anguilla onto the world scene. In a situation that parallels an early Peter Sellers movie, *The Mouse that Roared*, British paratroopers landed on Anguilla to prevent it from withdrawing from the Associated State Britain had established with Nevis and St. Kitts. Anguilla was an unwilling participant. In February of 1967, Anguilla evicted the St. Kittian police and set up its own government on Anguilla Day, May 30. The British sent an advisor to try and resolve the situation, but when he was unable to do so, the British Red Devils invaded the island. It took 10 more years for Anguilla to formally separate from St. Kitts-Nevis, but it remains an Associated State. It has a British Governor as well as a locally elected legislature.

The premise of *The Mouse that Roared* was that, after a war, Britain always rebuilds and enhances the vanquished country – and that is what happened here. New roads were built, as was the airport, and lots of long-overdue projects were completed.

As TV news broadcasts covered this "invasion," they showed the island and its world-class beaches. The tourist industry was born.

Anguilla's beaches are stunning. It has elegant resorts and over 50 good restaurants. It is a laid-back, informal destination and is a great spot for a honeymoon.

Getting There

By Boat

Ferries leave from the pier in Marigot for the 20-minute crossing to Blowing Point, Anguilla, every half-hour starting at 8 am. The last ferry leaves at 5:30 pm. Return ferries leave from 8:30 am until 5 pm. Late night ferries leave Marigot at 7 pm and 11 pm and Blowing Point at 6 pm and 9:15 pm. The fare is $10 each way and there is a $2 departure tax. Proof of citizenship is required.

By Air

You can fly into Princess Juliana Airport in Sint Maarten and connect to a commuter line for the seven-minute flight to **Wallblake Airport**. Winair, Air Anguilla and LIAT make this flight several times daily in season.

Anguilla

You can also fly to Puerto Rico and connect to American Eagle for the one-hour flight to the island.

The departure tax is $15.

Getting Around

Day-Trippers: A private taxi island tour costs $40.

Bicycles: Rent a bicycle at Blowing Point Ferry Terminal.

Car Rentals: Drive on the left.

Thrifty	☎ 264-497-2656
Island	☎ 264-497-2723
Hertz	☎ 264-497-2934
Connors	☎ 264-497-6433

Taxis: Taxis meet flights and ferries. There are no meters, but there is a flat, fixed rate.

The Beaches

Anguilla's beaches are truly prize-winning. There are dozens of them, all covered with beautiful white sand. Fronted by clear blue waters, the beaches are crescent-shaped and run as far as the eye can see. Some are backed by limestone cliffs, others have seagrape trees and waterfront centers. Still others house elegant resorts and restaurants. Many have coral reefs near the shore so snorkeling is easy and fun. Looking at a map of the island, you'll notice the overwhelming number of bays, points and harbors.

Shoal Bay East

This may be the best beach in the Caribbean. It stretches for a mile, has very clear water and a coral reef very near the shore. Hotels and restaurants are on the beach. Watersports and lounge chair rentals are offered.

Island Harbour Bay

Lined by coconut trees, this is home base for the brightly colored motor-powered fishing boats that bring in the day's catch of lobster and fish. There are restaurants here. Take the three-minute boat ride to Scilly Bay for snorkeling and lunch.

Rendezvous Bay

This 1½-mile beach has calm waters and is home to the Sonesta Beach Resort and smaller hotels and restaurants.

Barnes Bay

Cliffs line the bay and you'll have to climb down to the beach. The coral reef is close enough to the shore that you can see the multicolored fish darting through it. This is a great windsurfing beach. Watersports rentals and restaurants are offered.

Maundy's Bay

This popular beach is home to Cap Juluca Resort, once featured on *Lifestyles of the Rich and Famous* (see page 292). It is over one mile long. There's no coral reef here, but the beach is good for swimming and watersports (rentals available). Restaurant.

Shoal Bay West End

From Shoal Bay you can see St. Martin and the cruise ships in the distance. Snorkeling is excellent. Fishermen set nets on one end of the beach. Stop for conch fritters at Covecastles Restaurant.

Road Bay

(also called Sandy Ground)

Lots of yachts and sailboats anchor here. It is an excellent windsurfing and waterskiing beach. Watersports rentals.

Watersports

Scuba Diving

Scuba diving is well organized and the island offers both natural and man-made sites. They include coral fields, shipwrecks, underwater canyons, and cliff edges. Dives include night and photographic tours.

Anguillan Divers . . . . . ☎ 264-497-4750

Shoal Bay Scuba & Watersports . . . . ☎ 264-497-4371

Special "D" Diving & Boat Services . . . . ☎ 264-497-4567

Day Sails

Sails to an uninhabited cay or secluded beach, snorkel tours or fishing trips are offered by the following:

Chocolat . . . . ☎ 264-497-3394

No Mercy . . . . ☎ 264-235-6283

Island Yacht Charter Co. . . ☎ 264-497-3743

Once A Night . . . . ☎ 264-497-6109

Checkers Fun Tours . . . . ☎ 264-497-4071

Anguilla

Dolphin Fantasea

Here, participants can swim and interact with dolphins and stingrays. Trainers help you feed them and explain how the silky creatures live. Mead's Bay, ☎ 264-497-7946.

Marine Parks

In 1993, the Anguillan government created marine parks in an effort to protect the coral reef and segrass beds that were damaged by pleasure boats. There are five parks: **Dog Island**, **Prickly Pear Cay with Seal Island**, **Sandy Island**, **Little Bay and Shoal Bay** and **Island Harbour** reef system. There are fees to enter the parks and designated moorings. A dive permit is needed to scuba in the parks. Local tour operators have the necessary documents. If you have your own boat, stop in the Immigration and Customs office at the Blowing Point dock.

Boat Racing, Anguilla's National Passion

Part of Anguilla's history and its heritage are boat races that feature beautiful wooden sailboats. The tradition began a half-century ago when fishing boats were powered by wind. The desire to get home as quickly as possible led to a competition among the boats traveling together. Today's boats are handcrafted by crew members and represent different villages and clubs. There are three classes of boats, based on length and the number of crew members allowed. The courses vary and races are held throughout the year. The most important is held on Anguilla Day, May 30, when the entire island is circled. You can watch the start and finish from the appropriate beach, as do hundreds of locals. Between start and finish, there is live music and lots of food.

Land-Based Sports

Horseback Riding

A daily trail ride is offered at **El Rancho del Blues**, ☎ 264-497-6164.

Tennis

Peter Burwash International runs tennis programs throughout the Caribbean. Here, the company manages **Cap Juluca's** three courts and **Malliouhana's** four courts. There are courts at the **Sonesta Beach Resort, Enclave at Cinnamon Reef** and the **Fountain Beach and Tennis Club**. See pages 292-94 below for contacts.

Sunup to Sundown

Sightseeing

The Valley

At mid-island, The Valley is Anguilla's capital. **Wallblake Airport** is on the outskirts of the town, as is the old salt pond. The town has a half-dozen streets, schools, churches, local businesses and shops. In-town sights include:

Wallblake House: Built in 1787 with stone cut on the island's East End, it's a traditional plantation house with carved woodwork on its ceilings. The grounds have a cistern and a "bakery" that prepared meats. It's owned by the Catholic Church and services are held on the grounds.

Old Island House: The two-story wooden structure built in 1800 was renovated by a local family and painted apple green. It once housed magistrates but is now an art gallery.

Old Warden's Place: The traditional home of the island administrator and doctor is now a restaurant. The stone work here is impressive.

The Old Factory: Opposite Wallblake House, the factory produced island gin. It was originally part of the plantation.

Around The Island

Sand Hill: There is an old fort here where island defenders took refuge when the French attacked in 1796.

Island Harbor: This is a quaint fishing village where many residents are of Irish descent. The brightly painted boats often go 40 or 50 miles offshore to bring in lobsters and fish. A small museum about the Amerindians who lived on the island is on the grounds of the Arawak Beach Resort.

Crocus Hill Prison: On the island's highest point at 213 feet, the prison is in ruins but the view is fabulous.

Heritage Collection Museum: An array of archaeological and historical artifacts that span Anguillan history, from the Arawaks to the 1967 revolution. Relics, photos and old records allow visitors a peek at Anguilla and Anguillians. Monday-Saturday, 10-5. $5 admission charge.

Shop Till You Drop

Most serious shoppers hop the ferry to Marigot, but the upscale resorts have some interesting local shops and others are scattered through the island. Some choices follow:

Anguilla

Georgiana's, The Valley, sells local and regional crafts, T-shirts, jams, jellies and art.

Bartlett's Collections, Back Street in South Hill, sells similar items but has a more extensive selection of pottery and candles.

Irie Life, South Hill, sells colorful T-shirts, beachwear, hats and jams.

Best Places to Stay

Resorts

CuisinArt Resort & Spa
☎ 800-943-3210; www.cuisinartresort.com
Deluxe
Anguilla's newest deluxe resort. It's owned by the company that makes the popular kitchen tool. Accommodations are in tri-level buildings spread along the beach. The grounds are magnificent, with a large pool and tennis courts. The spa has a fitness center, as well as a variety of treatments. Cooking classes are offered.

Sonesta Anguilla Beach Resort
☎ 264-497-6999; fax 264-497-6899;
www.sonesta.com/anguilla
Expensive
Formerly the Casablanca Hotel, the Sonesta mixes white marble and colorful mosaics,

Moroccan arches and tropical gardens. Its beach runs for three miles, and the resort has a magnificent pool, fitness center, and tennis courts. Several restaurants.

Cap Juluca
☎ 888-858-5822; www.capjuluca.com
Deluxe
Cap Juluca is a complex of white moorish buildings along a two-mile beach. Accommodations include rooms, suites and villas. The resort has two restaurants, tennis courts, watersports center and fitness room.

Malliouhana
☎ 800-835-0796; fax 264-497-6011;
www.malliouhana.com
Deluxe
This stunning building with boutiques and restaurants sits on a hillside overlooking two beaches. Amenities include a watersports center, two swimming pools, tennis and fitness center.

Enclave at Cinnamon Reef
☎ 800-223-1108
Expensive
This "boutique" hotel has 22 suites, all recently renovated and refurbished by new owners. Facing Little Harbour Beach, the resort has tennis courts and a full watersports program.

Anguilla

Frangipani Beach Club
☎ 800-829-4564;
http://frangipani.ai/index_body.shtml
Expensive
Located on beautiful Mead's Bay, this 16-room stop has one of Anguilla's finest restaurants.

Tourist Board Information

There are many hotels and guest houses on the island. Information is available from the tourist board.

Anguilla Tourist Board, ☎ 264-497-2759; from the United States, ☎ 800-553-4939; fax 305-670-0040; atbtour@anguillanet.com.

Anguilla has small inns, apartments and villas for rent as well. Ask for the *Accommodations Rate Guide* at their office in the US, ☎ 267-880-3511, enterprisefx@aol.com, or contact one of these agencies:

Anguilla Connection Ltd., ☎ 800-916-3336, axconnect@anguillanet.com; **Elegant Retreats**, ☎ 264-497-2596, prems@anguillanet.com.

Best Places to Eat

Altamer Restaurant
Shoal Bay West
☎ 264-498-4040
Expensive
Subdued lighting, ocean views and innovative French cuisine make chef Maurice Leduc's place arguably the island's finest restaurant.

Corals
Mead's Bay Hideway (condo complex)
☎ 264-498-5555
Expensive
Part of a restaurant/shop complex, Corals sits under a thatch roof amid rock gardens. It serves Mediterranean fare from 11 am to 11 pm daily. Also in the complex, **The Lobster Bar** overlooks the dolphin pool and **The Ice Cream Shop** has 29 flavors of Italian gelato. A nice place to visit.

Tasty's Café
South Hill
☎ 264-497-2737
Moderate
The best Creole food on Anguilla is served at this small café. Conch, crayfish, curried goat and sautéed pork chops are house favorites. The menu changes daily to take advantage of the freshest ingredients.

Anguilla

Roy's Place
Crocus Bay
☎ 264-497-2470
Moderate
Lots of salads, burgers and fish 'n chips at lunch, but steak and lobster dominate the dinner menu. Lovely seaside restaurant.

Straw Hat
Forest Bay
☎ 264-497-8300
Expensive
Built on pilings extending into the bay, Straw Hat serves the island's freshest seafood in a casual dining room.

The Overlook
Back Street, South Hill
☎ 264-497-4488
Expensive
Jamaican-born and CIA-trained owner/chef Deon Thomas prepares Creole cuisine, including his signature dish, garlic-crusted red snapper. Very informal.

Smokeys at the Cove
Cove Bay
☎ 264-497-6582
Moderate
A stylish bistro that serves lots of local dishes, such as African chicken wings with a five-spice sauce, honeyed baby ribs and spicy seafood chowder.

Blanchards'
Meads Bay
☎ 264-497-6100
Expensive
On the waterfront, Blanchards' serves Cajun, Caribbean and Asian specialties. Extensive wine cellar. Dinner only.

Hibernia
Island Harbour
☎ 264-497-4290
Moderate
The chef studied in Bangkok and many specialties are Southeast Asian. Others are French and include duck and local seafood.

Uncle Ernie's
Shoal Bay
Inexpensive
A local hangout with inexpensive beer, Creole food and live music on weekends. Open 10 am to 8 pm.

Nightlife

Most evening diversions are centered around the resort hotels and restaurants. Check with the hotel concierge for special events. Reggae, steel bands and barbecues are popular. **Johnno's** on Sandy Ground (☎ 264-497-2728) and its neighbor, the **Pumphouse** (☎ 264-497-5154), often have reggae.

Anguilla

Index

www.hunterpublishing.com

Hunter's full range of travel guides to all corners of the globe is featured on our exciting web site. You'll find guidebooks to suit every type of traveler, no matter what their budget, lifestyle, or idea of fun. Full descriptions are given for each book, along with reviewers' comments and a cover image. Books may be purchased on-line using a credit card via our secure transaction system.

Alive Guides featured include *Aruba, Bonaire & Curaçao; Cancún & Cozumel; Hollywood & the Best of Los Angeles; Dominica & St. Lucia; Antigua, Barbuda, St. Kitts & Nevis; Cayman Islands; Long Island;* and *The US Virgin Islands*.

Check out our *Adventure Guides*, a series aimed at the independent traveler with a focus on outdoor activities (rafting, hiking, biking, skiing, etc.). All books in this signature series cover places to stay and eat, sightseeing, in-town attractions, transportation and more!

Hunter's *Romantic Weekends* series offers myriad things to do for couples of all ages and lifestyles. Quaint places to stay and restaurants where the ambiance will take your breath away are included, along with fun activities that you and your partner will remember forever.

HUNTER TRAVEL GUIDES

www.hunterpublishing.com

Hunter's full range of travel guides to all corners of the globe is featured on our exciting Web site. You'll find guidebooks to suit every type of traveler, no matter what their budget, lifestyle, or idea of fun. Full descriptions are given for each book, along with reviewers' comments and a cover image. Books may be purchased on-line using a credit card via our secure transaction system. All on-line orders receive a 20% discount.

ALIVE! GUIDES

Alive! guides tell you what's hot, and what's not, with plenty of suggestions for daytime activity and nighttime fun. Hundreds of restaurant and hotel profiles in all price ranges, including the best places to stay and eat if you're looking for pampering, adventure, nights in the city or value. Beyond where to stay and eat, *Alive!* guides focus on the things that make each destination unique – from scenic fall drives on Long Island to spectacular rain forest lodges in Costa Rica. There are full details about local celebrations, along with contact numbers for help in trip-planning. "Sun-up to Sundown" sections describe daytime activities from sightseeing and swimming to shopping and beachcombing. "After Dark" sections give the lowdown on nightlife from mild

to wild. An "A-Z" section provides a comprehensive list of useful contacts, including ATM and bank locations, doctors and medical facilities, tourism offices, religious services and web sites. All have town and regional maps, in-margin icons, and are indexed.

Alive! guides featured include: *Antigua, Barbuda, St. Kitts & Nevis; Aruba, Bonaire & Curaçao; Atlanta; Baltimore & The Chesapeake Bay; Bermuda; Bucks County & The Delaware River Valley; Buenos Aires & The Best of Argentina; Cancún &*

Cozumel; *The Catskills*; *Dallas & Fort Worth*; *Dominica & St. Lucia*; *Hollywood & The Best of Los Angeles*; *Jamaica*; *Long Island*; *Martinique & Guadeloupe*; *Martinique, Guadeloupe, Dominica & St. Lucia*; *Miami & The Florida Keys*; *Nassau & The Best of the Bahamas*; *St. Martin & St. Barts*; and *Venezuela*.

ADVENTURE GUIDES

Adventure Guides are aimed at the independent traveler who enjoys outdoor activities (rafting, hiking, biking, skiing, canoeing, etc.). All books in this signature series cover places to stay and eat, sightseeing, in-town attractions, transportation and more!

With over 30 titles, the *Adventure Guide* series is recognized as a top resource for active travelers, whether your idea of fun is rock climbing, beachcombing or cycling. Each book offers the ideal mix of practical travel information along with activities. And the fun is for everyone, no matter your age or ability level. Never galloped along a beach on horseback before? Check out the lists of recommended outfitters and training stables and give it a go! Have you always yearned to see the colorful marine life below the water's surface? *Adventure Guides* list plenty of diver certification courses to get you started, plus the best sites once you're ready to take the plunge.

Comprehensive background information – history, culture, geography and climate – gives you a solid knowledge of your destination, its people and their roots. Regional chapters take you on an introductory tour, with stops at museums, historic sites and local attractions. Then come the adventures – fishing, canoeing, water skiing, rafting, llama trips, snowboarding and more. There are sections detailing places to stay and eat; transportation to, from and around your destination; practical concerns; useful web sites; e-mail addresses; and tourism contacts. Detailed regional and town maps feature walking and driving tours, historic sites, attractions, and parks. All guides in the series are fully indexed. Photographs enhance the lively text.

ROMANTIC WEEKENDS

Hunter's *Romantic Weekends* series offers myriad things to do for couples of all ages and lifestyles. Quaint places to stay and restaurants where the ambiance will take your breath away are included, along with fun activities that you and your partner will remember forever.

The ultimate series for romancers of all ages and lifestyles, with ideas to suit every budget. These books offer much more than just a listing of intimate restaurants with candlelit tables – the focus is also on fun activities that you and your partner can enjoy together. Beautiful places to stay, charming spots to eat and unusual things to do allow you to plan a unique weekend getaway. Savor wines at a local vineyard, have a five-star dinner delivered to your room and stay in for the evening, visit museums and quaint coffeehouses, stroll arm-in-arm under the stars, or enjoy a secluded picnic with champagne. These inspiring guidebooks will help you decide where, why and how you want to treat yourselves. Hunter's *Romantic Weekends* books make fine gifts for weddings and anniversaries, too!

LANDMARK VISITORS GUIDES

Touring itineraries take you through towns and villages, into the countryside to some of the best beaches. You'll visit museums, historic buildings, beautiful churches and perhaps stop to join in local celebrations. Interesting tidbits are highlighted in colorful callout boxes, and might tell how the landscape has been shaped, which birds you can expect to see, or where the best
fishing spot is. Whether you're planning your first trip or are a veteran traveler, don't leave home without a Landmark Visi-

tors Guide, renowned as the best choice for sightseers. Lavish color throughout, plus detailed maps.

NELLES GUIDES

These great-value guides cover destinations far and wide around the globe. Established in 1990, *Nelles Guides* sought to provide travelers with comprehensive destination coverage in a handy, take-along format. Today, the tradition continues. Nelles Guides are researched and written by local correspondents and are updated regularly. Each book has a well-rounded introduction that delves into the country's history and culture, tempting the reader to explore.

The "What to See & Do" section for each area can cover anything from sightseeing and driving tours to jungle treks and visits to the local museums. You'll find detailed entries for restaurants, shopping, entertainment, festivals and more. All accommodations are categorized by price level, making it easy for the reader to select a place to suit his/her budget. Practical travel issues – health concerns, climate and clothing, visa requirements, currency, transportation, etc. – are also addressed. Priced at just $15.95 and packed with over 160 color photos per book, the value is unbeatable!

THIS WAY GUIDES

A remarkable series of handy pocket-size guides to take with you as you explore Prague, Amsterdam, Alaska, Florence, Munich, Vienna and even Tahiti. With stunning color photos and high-quality fold-out maps in back, they offer unbeatable value at just $5.95. Their durable design and light weight means you can tote them along all day, referring to them as often as you need. *This Way* guides provide travelers with a maximum of cultural, historical and practical information in the smallest package possible, directing you on walking tours to attractions and sights that you simply can't afford to miss. Historic buildings, the best museums, delightful parks and plazas – all are described and come with comprehensive directions for easy access on foot or by local transport systems. The "Dining Out" sections offer a good selection of places to eat, covering all kinds of cuisines and ensuring a pleasant meal for everyone, even the kids. Each book features a "Hard Facts" section that shows basic travel information at a glance – post office hours, pharmacies, driving and car hire concerns, tipping policies, tourist information offices, travel options and a list of recommended guides and tour operators. Up-to-date, authoritative and easy to use, these are the guides to take with you!

TRAVEL NOTES

_____

_____

_____

_____

_____

_____

_____

_____

_____

_____

_____

_____

_____

_____

_____

_____

_____

_____

_____

TRAVEL NOTES

_____
_____
_____
_____
_____
_____
_____
_____
_____
_____
_____
_____
_____
_____
_____
_____
_____
_____
_____

TRAVEL NOTES

_____

_____

_____

_____

_____

_____

_____

_____

_____

_____

_____

_____

_____

_____

_____

_____

_____

_____

_____

_____

TRAVEL NOTES

_____

_____

_____

_____

_____

_____

_____

_____

_____

_____

_____

_____

_____

_____

_____

_____

_____

_____

TRAVEL NOTES

TRAVEL NOTES

_____

_____

_____

_____

_____

_____

_____

_____

_____

_____

_____

_____

_____

_____

_____

_____

_____

_____

TRAVEL NOTES

_____

_____

_____

_____

_____

_____

_____

_____

_____

_____

_____

_____

_____

_____

_____

_____

_____

_____

TRAVEL NOTES

_____

_____

_____

_____

_____

_____

_____

_____

_____

_____

_____

_____

_____

_____

_____

_____

_____

_____

_____

_____

TRAVEL NOTES

_____

_____

_____

_____

_____

_____

_____

_____

_____

_____

_____

_____

_____

_____

_____

_____

_____

_____

TRAVEL NOTES

_____

_____

_____

_____

_____

_____

_____

_____

_____

_____

_____

_____

_____

_____

_____

_____

_____

TRAVEL NOTES

_____

_____

_____

_____

_____

_____

_____

_____

_____

_____

_____

_____

_____

_____

_____

_____

_____

_____

TRAVEL NOTES

_____

_____

_____

_____

_____

_____

_____

_____

_____

_____

_____

_____

_____

_____

_____

_____

_____

TRAVEL NOTES

TRAVEL NOTES

_____

_____

_____

_____

_____

_____

_____

_____

_____

_____

_____

_____

_____

_____

_____

_____

_____

TRAVEL NOTES